IN
THE COURT OF PUBLIC OPINION
FOR THE PEOPLE OF THE UNITED STATES

	(
	(
	(
	(THE CASE FOR
	(WAR CRIMES
INDICTMENT:	(AGAINST THE
	(GEORGE W BUSH
	(ADMINISTRATION
	(
	(

By
Joel F. Russell

ISBN 978-0692890233
© Copyright 2017 Joel F. Russell
Clarity Publishing Services
Flagstaff, Arizona

We too often bind ourselves by authorities rather than by the truth.
        –Lucretia Mott

TABLE OF CONTENTS

FORWARD.. 1

OPENING ARGUMENTS... 5

HISTORICAL BACKGROUND 9

PART 1: THE WAR... 13

    Shock & Awe: The Invasion... 13

    The Fall of Baghdad.. 16

    The Occupation 17

    The Insurgency... 20

    The Surge 23

    Sunni Awakening... 24

    Drawdown of US Troops 25

    Iraq Today 27

PART 2: THE CASE 31

    The Charges 31

    What the Administration Said 32

    Bringing Down Saddam 35

    Attempts to Provoke a Fight with Iraq.. 37

    Propaganda Machine 38

    Pre-Invasion Actions and Troop Movements............................. 40

    Weapons of Mass Destruction 41

        Mobile Biological Weapons Factories 42

        Nigerien Uranium Ore.. 50

        Aluminum Tubes... 53

    Terrorist Connections 55

    Regime Change 57

    Motivation 58

        Revenge 58

        Oil.. 59

        A Long-term Military Presence 62

        Projecting American Power: PNAC 64

    Conclusions 67

CLOSING ARGUMENTS... 69

AFTERWORD 77

APPENDIX: THE DEFENDANTS... 81

FORWARD

Prior to the invasion of Iraq in 2003, the Unites States had gone to war at least three times under very dubious circumstances.

The first was in 1846, when America went to war with Mexico. The US sent troops to the Rio Grande after Mexico rebuffed attempts by President James K. Polk to purchase territory. The United States claimed that the river was the international border; Mexico, which claimed all of Texas, attacked the American troops. The US declared war and quickly defeated the much weaker Mexican army. In the 1848 Treaty of Guadalupe Hidalgo, Mexico ceded Upper California and the New Mexico territory to the United States, along with Texas, adding some 900,000 square miles to the country. Many prominent Americans, including Abraham Lincoln and Ulysses S Grant, declared that it was a very transparent war of territorial acquisition.

Then in 1898, the United States went to war with Spain, a war in which the country gained several overseas possessions. In the late 1890s, competing newspapers began printing anti-Spanish propaganda and calls for war amid small revolts against Spanish rule in Cuba. When the battleship *Maine* exploded and sank in Havana harbor, the same newspapers claimed it was deliberately sunk by the Spanish, and the US declared war. The war was ostensibly about Cuban independence, but when the US defeated Spain after ten weeks of fighting, it gained possession of Cuba, plus Puerto Rico and The Philippines. Cuba remained in US possession until after World War II, and we fought a bloody, four-year guerilla war against the Filipinos, who wrongly assumed that we were there to liberate them. The Philippines eventually won its independence, but the United States maintained large military bases there until recently. Later investigations revealed that the *Maine* was most likely sunk by a boiler explosion, not the Spanish.

In 1964, the American destroyer USS *Maddox* was reportedly attacked twice by North Vietnamese torpedo boats in the Gulf of Tonkin, off the coast of North Vietnam. President Lyndon Johnson seized on this incident as an excuse to greatly expand American military operations in Southeast Asia. Rather than being a war of territorial acquisition, the Vietnam debacle was a proxy war with the Soviet Union, and an attempt to block the spread of Communism in that part of the world. But it was also sold on false pretenses; in the first attack, the US claimed the Vietnamese fired first, but in actuality, it was the *Maddox*, which was in North Vietnamese waters, that fired first. And, according to then-Secretary of Defense Robert McNamara, the second incident never happened. The US fought for ten years in Vietnam, costing some 58,000 Americans their lives.

In each of these wars, the public was misled in the government's rush to go to war, before cooler heads could put a damper on the war fever.

When the Administration of George W Bush started agitating for an invasion of Iraq, I did not think of unprovoked wars started on false pretenses. What I thought was, "Iraq? *Iraq?!*" I thought we were at war with the al Qaida terrorists responsible for the 9/11 attacks, and the Taliban who sheltered them in Afghanistan. What did Iraq have to with anything?

When it became obvious to me that Bush and company were serious about starting another war in Iraq, I thought, "No, no, no, you can't invade Iraq; you will set off a civil war between the Sunnis and Shiites, and American soldiers are going to get caught right in the middle of it. This, of course, is exactly what

2

happened. I also expected the Kurds in the north of Iraq to rebel, starting a general Kurdish insurrection that would destabilize the entire region. That, as we know, didn't happen, but the invasion of Iraq was none the less at least partially responsible for the instability that we see in the Middle East today.

But I thought, surely someone in the Administration must see the dangers inherent in invading Iraq and deposing dictator Saddam Hussein. Surely calmer voices of reason will prevail, and the Administration will change its tune. But, as we all know, this did not happen. I was left to wonder, what were Bush and his administration thinking? Iraq was not overtly threatening the United States, not in any way that would seem to require an immediate invasion. And why start another war when we were already involved in a foreign war? What was so important about Iraq? Why did they have to invade that country, and why was an invasion considered so urgent?

It made no sense to me. All of a sudden, out of nowhere, Iraq is suddenly the biggest threat we faced, according to the Bush Administration. What were they up to?

INDICTMENT

OPENING ARGUMENTS

May it please the Court of Public Opinion:
Ladies and gentlemen of the jury: we intend to prove that the administration of President George W. Bush did willfully and maliciously mislead the American people into accepting a war of choice, not a war of necessity.

The war in Iraq was ill conceived and ill advised. It was a war with no clear objectives other than deposing a dictator, and a war with a nation that was not threatening the United States in any way, shape, or form. It was a war that was justified on allegations for which there was no credible evidence. It was a war in which the American people were deliberately deceived about the need to expend American lives and treasure. It was a war that the Bush Administration intended to prosecute despite any opposition. In a nutshell, George Bush et al. decided to invade Iraq, and then went looking for a rationale that the American population would accept.

We, the prosecution, also charge that the Bush Administration did cynically take advantage of the fears Americans felt after the 9/11 terrorist attacks in order to convince Americans that they faced grave danger from Iraq, which, in fact, they did not.

We charge specifically that the George W. Bush Administration deliberately misled the American public about their reasons for this invasion, making false claims about the need to go to war, while masking their actual, ideologically driven objectives.

We do not make these charges lightly, for we know what the implications of a guilty verdict are. A guilty verdict would mean that all those lives were lost for a lie; all that taxpayer money was wasted on a lie. All the blood, sweat, and tears were expended for no good reason. It would mean that thousands of families, both American and Iraqi, would have salt rubbed in their wounds by the knowledge that their loved ones died in a war prosecuted under false pretenses. These poor people would understand that their loved ones did not have to die, that they should not have died. They will realize that their loved ones died or were maimed because the government lied to us.

In addition, a guilty verdict would severely damage the international reputation of the United States, and could even lead to serious calls for the prosecution of Bush et al. for war crimes in an international court.

None the less, these charges must be laid, for, painful as it may be, the American people deserve to know the truth, if for no other reason, that we may resolve ourselves not to allow our government to wage unnecessary wars in the future.

Therefore, the prosecution intends to prove that President George W. Bush, Vice President Richard Cheney, Secretary of Defense Donald Rumsfeld, Assistant Secretary of Defense Paul Wolfowitz, among others, did deliberately mislead the American people into accepting a war on false premises, to wit:

They claimed to have proof that Iraq possessed weapons of mass destruction; they had no such proof.

They claimed that Saddam Hussein was providing material support to Osama bin Laden, when the two were actually sworn enemies.

They claimed, when the former allegations proved false, that they were bringing democracy to Iraq; this from an administration that had, from the beginning, declared it was not going to get into nation building.

The prosecution also intends to prove that the Bush administration did have motives for the invasion of Iraq, but ones that they did not share with the American people, because the American people would have rejected such motives.

We feel confident that the evidence we present will convince you, the jury in this Court of Public Opinion, that the Bush government is in fact guilty of war crimes for their unwarranted invasion of Iraq.

But before we present our case, we must examine the events in question, along with a little historical background.

INDICTMENT

HISTORICAL BACKGROUND

The modern state of Iraq was created from the ashes of the Ottoman Empire following the end of the First World War. The victorious allies carved up the Middle East, creating, among others nations, the Protectorate of Iraq. Iraq gained full independence as a kingdom in 1932. The military overthrew the monarchy in 1958 and established a republic.

The Ba'ath Party was created in the early 1950s as a largely Shiite, pan-Arab group, but soon became majority Sunni. The Ba'ath overthrew the ruling party in Iraq in 1963; a counter-coup drove the Ba'athists underground, but the party retook power in another coup in 1968. Saddam Hussein wrested control of the party, and Iraq, in 1979. Saddam and his Sunni-led party ruled with a heavy hand, repressing the country's Shiite majority until being overthrown by the US-led invasion in 2003.

Relations between Iraq and neighboring Iran remained reasonably friendly until the Ba'ath Party came to power in Iraq. Iran abrogated the Shatt-al-Arab waterway treaty in 1969; Iraq broke off diplomatic relations with Iran over another territorial dispute in 1971. Iran began to support Kurdish separatist rebels in the north of Iraq; Iraq reciprocated by arming both Kurdish and Baluchistan rebels in Iran. However, a treaty managed to keep the peace for a while.

But after the 1979 Islamic revolution in Iran, new Iranian leader Ayatollah Ruhollah Khomeini urged the Iraqis to overthrow their Ba'athist government. Tensions mounted between the secularist, Sunni-led Iraqi government and the new, Shiite theocracy next door.

Iran's new religious leaders conducted a purge of the military, which, along with a lack of spare parts, greatly weakened Iran's defense forces. Thinking that he could take advantage of this weakness, Iraqi dictator Saddam Hussein decided to attack. Iraq invaded Iran without warning in September 1980 (with covert American encouragement). But the Iraqi army failed to advance very far into Iran, and by 1981 the war had evolved into a stalemate, with neither side able to take the advantage. The war would drag on for eight bloody years.

For most of the war, the United States government sided with Iraq, even after Iranian diplomats presented evidence to the United Nations that Iraq was using chemical weapons against Iran. President Reagan sent former (and future) Secretary of Defense Donald Rumsfeld to Iraq to assure Saddam Hussein of America's continued support, while the Administration publically denounced Iraq's use of chemical weapons. Meanwhile, the US provided Iraq with intelligence and other material support. Reagan also induced Saudi Arabia to transfer military hardware to Iraq, which Saddam Hussein used to step up his air strikes on Iran.

But at the same time, the Reagan Administration concocted a deal in which they sold arms to Iran in exchange for the release of American hostages held by the Iranian-backed Hezbollah militia in Lebanon. This plan evolved into the Iran-Contra scandal that plagued the second term of the Reagan Administration.

In 1988, Iran began to sue for peace after Iraq stepped up its air attacks, including a poison gas attack that killed or wounded more than 2,000 civilians. In August 1988 the two sides agreed to a United Nations resolution calling for an end to the war, although low level fighting between the two countries continued for several more years. A peace treaty was finally signed in 1990. The Iran-Iraq War was devastating to both nations; the death toll, both civilian and military, was in the hundreds of thousands. The financial toll was estimated to be in the neighborhood of $500 million for each nation.

But Saddam Hussein was not done fighting with his neighbors. He asserted that the bordering emirate of Kuwait rightfully belonged to Iraq. He also accused Kuwait of stealing oil from a field on the border between the two states. After months of threats and saber rattling, Iraq invaded in Kuwait in August of 1990. It took two days for Saddam to defeat the Kuwaiti military; the government and royal family fled, and Iraqi forces occupied all of Kuwait. Saddam Hussein declared Kuwait to be an Iraqi province and appointed his cousin as governor.

The United Nations and the Arab League called for Iraq to withdraw from Kuwait, but Saddam Hussein resisted all diplomatic efforts to end the crisis. When he began to threaten Saudi Arabia, whose major oil fields adjoin Kuwait, Saudi Arabia asked the United States for help. Then-President George H.W. Bush sent troops to the desert kingdom under the codename Operation Desert Shield. Bush then assembled a 34-nation coalition, largely thanks to the peripatetic efforts of Secretary of State James Baker. A huge, multinational force was assembled, with about 75% of the troops being American.

The campaign, dubbed Operation Desert Storm, began in January 1991 with what has been described as the most intensive air bombardment in military history. In February, US troops entered Kuwait from Saudi Arabia while forces from Arab states entered from the east. The Iraqi forces did not put up much of a fight, with many surrendering after only token resistance. After the liberation of Kuwait City, Saddam Hussein ordered a withdrawal from Kuwait. Coalition forces chased the Iraqis, who set the Kuwaiti oil fields on fire on their way out, back across the border and into Iraq. The coalition troops pursued the Iraqi army to within 150 miles of Baghdad, while aerial bombardment killed hundreds of the retreating Iraqi forces. The coalition troops eventually retreated back to the Saudi and Kuwaiti borders, and President Bush called a ceasefire on February 28.

Believing the United States would back them up after comments made by Bush, the so-called marsh Arabs in the south and the Kurds in the north of Iraq rebelled against Saddam Hussein. But Saddam brutally crushed these rebellions, which got no help from the US or its allies. However, the coalition did establish no-fly zones in the north and south of the country, in which coalition aircraft patrolled the skies in order to protect the minorities in these areas from Saddam Hussein.

Subsequently, the United Nations passed resolutions barring Iraq from developing or possessing chemical, biological, or nuclear weapons. Inspectors from the United Nations and the International Atomic Energy Agency began the process of finding and destroying Iraq's weapons of mass destruction in 1991. After seven years the inspectors left. The United Nations Special Commission on Iraq estimated that 90% to 95% of its weapons of mass destruction, along with delivery systems, had been destroyed. Weapons inspector Scott Ritter said in 1999, "Iraq today possesses no meaningful weapons of mass destruction capability."

PART 1: THE WAR

Shock & Awe: The Invasion

On Thursday, March 20th, 2003, the United States of America commenced a heavy bombardment of Baghdad, Iraq, a city of five million people. Hundreds of missiles were fired at Baghdad from US naval task forces in the Persian Gulf and the Red Sea. Huge explosions rocked the city, sending smoke and flames high into the air. Much of the southern part of the city was burning; towering flames were reflected in the Tigris River, along with the billowing smoke. Tracer bullets crisscrossed in the air, lighting up the early morning sky. US military leaders referred to this attack–ostensibly opening a new front in the war on terror–as "Shock & Awe."

President George W. Bush announced: "At this hour, American and coalition forces are in the early stages of military operations to disarm Iraq, to free its people and to defend the world from grave danger,"[1] while allied troops crossed the border from Kuwait, advancing deep into Iraq on the first day.

The Iraq War had begun.

The Administration had begun beating the war drums the previous September when Bush gave a speech to the United Nations General Assembly. Bush declared that Iraqi dictator Saddam Hussein was in violation of commitments he made at the end of the 1991 Gulf War. Most significantly, Bush declared that Saddam Hussein was expanding chemical weapons production and was continuing "to shelter and support terrorist organizations."[2] The Bush Administration began to seek UN approval for an invasion, while also trying to provoke a fight with Saddam Hussein.

This strident call to arms was not met with universal approbation. Several US allies refused to participate, most notably France and Germany, on the grounds that there was not enough evidence to justify an invasion. Angry public protests against a war were staged, not just in America, but around the world, also. However, the Bush Administration continued to push its case, insisting that we had to invade Iraq before it was too late. Indeed, both George W. Bush and his then-national security advisor, Condoleezza Rice, warned that we couldn't wait until the "smoking gun" came in the "form of a mushroom cloud."[3]

The United Nations, after much debate, refused to authorize an invasion. As a compromise, the UN resolved to resume weapons inspections in Iraq, a plan to which Saddam Hussein agreed. While the inspections were ongoing, the US Congress, in response to a request from the White House, passed a resolution authorizing the Bush Administration to use the US military "as he determines to be necessary " against the Iraqi regime.[4] In February 2003, United Nations weapons inspectors reported that they had found no evidence of any current program to develop and produce weapons of mass destruction.[5]

Regardless, the Administration continued to lead the nation headlong into war. On March 17, 2003, Bush gave Saddam Hussein and his sons Uday and Qusay 48 hours to surrender power and leave Iraq. When Saddam did not respond, Shock & Awe began.

Operations actually started before Bush's deadline for Saddam to leave Iraq. Intelligence on March 19th suggested that Saddam Hussein and his sons were at Dora Farms, a location on the outskirts of Baghdad. Military planners sent missiles and "bunker buster" bombs slamming into the compound. The strike was ineffectual; Saddam and his sons were not there. This was not the only failure of US intelligence in Iraq, as we shall see.

The bombardment of Baghdad continued for days, along with strikes on Mosul and Kirkuk, in northern Iraq. Meanwhile, having helped secure the Rumeila oil field before Saddam could torch it, the US 3rd Marine Division advanced on Nasiriyah, a strategically located city some 200 miles southeast of Baghdad. Heavy fighting in and around Nasiriyah resulted in many casualties, including thirty-two Americans killed.[6] Among those killed in action was Specialist Lori Piestewa, a Hopi from Tuba City, Arizona; Piestewa is believed to be the first Native American woman killed in combat in a foreign war.[7] On March 24th Iraqi forces launched a counterattack, which the Marines repelled, with air support. An estimated 200 to 300 Iraqis were killed without a single US casualty. Nasiriyah was declared secure the next morning.

While US forces were advancing on Nasiriyah, British forces met heavier than expected resistance as they began an assault on Basra, Iraq's second largest city, in the southern delta. It took two weeks of fighting to clear opposition forces from the city, including the largest tank battle British troops had engaged in since World War II. By April 6th the British had control over Basra.

American troops advanced up the Euphrates River valley toward the city of Najaf, where fighting commenced with a helicopter gunship assault, which met heavy resistance. On March 29th the US 101st Airborne Division began an attack on Najaf; with support from other divisions, they beat back stubborn opposition and finally took the city on April 4th.

About sixty miles south of Baghdad is the Karbala Gap, between the Euphrates River and Lake Razazah. This gap is the land route from southern Iraq to Baghdad, so it was strategically very important to Iraqi commanders, who positioned elite Republican Guard troops to block it. However, coalition forces had been conducting a deception designed to convince the Iraqis that the main invasion would come from the north, through Turkey. The ruse worked; Qusay Hussein ordered troops to redeploy to the north of Baghdad, over the objections of the Karbala area commander. American troops poured through the

15

gap and advanced to the Euphrates River town of Musayib. There they seized a bridge across the Euphrates after the Iraqis had failed to demolish it.

Troops from two Iraqi Armored Brigades launched an artillery-supported attack; it was countered with tank and artillery fire that destroyed every tank in the Iraqi assault. The next morning Coalition aircraft attacked the Iraqi positions, which crumbled, and US troops poured through the broken Iraqi lines, with not much between them and Baghdad.

The Fall of Baghdad

Three weeks after the invasion began, American and allied troops entered the Iraqi capital. On the morning of April 3rd, US forces advanced all the way to the Baghdad airport, which they secured after several hours of combat. Two days later, units of the US Third Infantry began what was called a "Thunder Run," a drive through the city to the airport, largely to test remaining Iraqi resistance. The Marines met with very little. Another Thunder Run started on April 7th that bypassed Iraqi reinforcements along the original Thunder Run route, instead pushing into the government district of the city.[8]

Also on April 7th Coalition forces engaged in operations to secure three main highway intersections. It took eighteen hours of fighting at the southern interchange, leading to two US KIA and hundreds of Iraqi casualties.

Although the city was far from totally secured, the allies declared on April 9th that Baghdad was formally occupied. Saddam Hussein disappeared from Baghdad on that same day. By April 12th the war was largely over.

Even though sectarian fighting in Iraq had already begun, George W. Bush declared an end to major combat operations on May 1st, after a dramatic landing on the deck of the aircraft carrier USS *Abraham Lincoln*.[9] A banner strung across the carrier's superstructure read "Mission Accomplished."

The Occupation

Saddam Hussein's military had been severely weakened after the devastating, decade long war with Iran, Operation Desert Storm in 1991, and years of Western sanctions. So there was never really any question that the world's most powerful military would roll over Saddam's forces. That was the easy part. The next part would prove to be far more problematic, to say the least.

From the beginning, there was resistance to the American occupation. Bush and company claimed that we were there as liberators; in fact, vice-president Dick Cheney had declared that the Iraqi populace would welcome us as such (wrong again).[10] But to many observers in the Middle East, our occupation of Iraq was proof of American aggression and imperialism. By the time US troops secured Baghdad, Islamists were already calling for jihad.

Some American officials wanted to get the United Nations involved in post-war Iraq, but Cheney and Secretary of Defense Donald Rumsfeld–who didn't even want the State Department involved–argued that the UN would only get in the way. An international coalition would not only have spread the cost among the allies, but it may also have put other countries in the region at ease regarding US intentions in Iraq, and perhaps may have softened opposition to the occupation. But that would not have given the administration the control it wanted. Cheney and Rumsfeld wanted a totally American occupation, with a hand-off directly to the Iraqis when the situation allowed it.[11]

Administration officials declared that the Iraqi government and other infrastructure would remain intact, and the occupation would last no more than 60 days. They also said that Iraq could finance its own reconstruction through oil revenues. Once again, administration predictions would prove to be way off the mark. Cheney and Rumsfeld might have known better if they had consulted with the State Department, but the Bush administration neoconservatives scorned State and did not want it to be involved in the occupation efforts.

The Bush administration first put retired Lt General Jay Garner in charge of these efforts, but he quickly fell into disfavor. He was blamed for the chaos and was considered too friendly with the Iraqis. In May 2003, Bush replaced Garner with Paul Bremer, a former aide to Henry Kissinger and a counterterrorism expert.

Even though he was a career diplomat, in Iraq Bremer was under the direct control of Defense Secretary Donald Rumsfeld, rather than the State Department. Only five days after arriving in Iraq, Bremer announced that he was dismantling the Ba'ath Party bureaucracy and the Army. What's more, Iraqi soldiers would not be paid money owed to them. When told by the CIA that these actions were going to create a lot of enemies for the American occupiers, Bremer replied that he had no choice. "Those are my instructions," he said.[12] As a result of these decisions, there was no one other than the US military to fight the mushrooming chaos, looting, and lawlessness, and there weren't enough forces to do the job. Government employees and soldiers found themselves out of a job, even if they were not members of Saddam's ruling Ba'ath Party.

Bremer soon realized his mistakes and tried to change course and reconstitute the army and police, even if it meant hiring former Ba'athists. Indeed, eventually, most of the officers of the new Iraqi Army would come from the old Iraqi Army. But it was too late; many disgruntled, former Party members had already joined the jihadists in opposing the American occupation, including many former Iraqi soldiers who took their weapons with them.

Administration officials also apparently did not understand the preexisting sectarian tensions in Iraq, and how the fall of Saddam Hussein's repressive government would release all that tension, leading to years of bloody fighting.

Conditions in Iraq quickly devolved into sectarian violence, attacks on American troops, and looting on a massive scale, which the US occupation forces seemed powerless to control. In fact, US military leaders had warned the Bush government that they did not have enough troops in Iraq to effectively secure the country without help from the Iraqi army and police. But the Bush administration hadn't really thought out what would happen after the invasion. They had no plan, but, as one White House official said, they were making it up as they went along.[13]

But the Administration wasn't totally winging it. Bush and Bremer had previously envisioned a 3-year process to write a constitution and then hold national elections, but, in the interest of extracting themselves from the growing quagmire, they decided that some form of Iraqi government had to be instituted as soon as possible. So in July of 2003, the American-led Coalition Provisional Authority (CPA) created the Iraqi Governing Council, a group composed mostly of Shiites, but also a few Sunnis and Kurds, and one Turkmen and an Assyrian. The Governing Council would function under the direct supervision of the CPA. The Governing Council was tasked with filling cabinet posts and drafting an interim constitution. The constitution the Council drafted called for a new, sovereign government to be in place by July 1, 2004.

Despite contentious debates between all the Iraqi factions, the Governing Council signed the interim constitution on March 8, 2004. The constitution called for the creation of a national parliament; elections for this National Assembly were held in January of 2005, amid deadly attacks by insurgents and others opposed to the elections. Despite the violence, turnout was heavy in Shiite and Kurdish districts; Sunnis stayed away in droves, threatening the legitimacy of the elections.

But faced with the prospect of living under a Shiite government, Sunni politicians offered to help draft the nation's permanent constitution, while Sunni insurgents continued to threaten anyone who participated in what they saw as the government of foreign occupiers.

The Iraqi Transitional Government, which was approved by the National Assembly in April, replaced the Iraqi Governing Council in May of 2005. At the same time the Coalition Provisional Authority was dissolved, leaving Iraqis in charge of their own government, at least on paper, for the first time in more than two years. Still, there were 135,000 US military personnel in Iraq at the time, and they were very busy trying to put a lid on the growing violence, not just against Americans, but between Sunnis and Shiites, as well.

The Insurgency

After the death of the prophet Mohammed in 632 CE, his followers split over who should succeed him, the prophet's father-in-law Abu Bakr or his son-in-law Ali Ibn Abi Talib. The dispute led to the formation of two sects within Islam, the Shia and the Sunni. The overwhelming majority of Muslims the world over belong to the Sunni sect; Saddam Hussein, along with his Ba'athist government and Republican Guards, were Sunni. However, Iraq is majority Shiite, and Saddam's minority government brutally repressed the majority. Removing the Sunnis from power was bound to lead to calls for vengeance from Shiite Iraqis who had long suffered at the hands of the Ba'athist regime. As the Bush government should have anticipated, sectarian strife began almost as soon as the Ba'athist government was overthrown.

The Sunni minority, which had controlled Iraq since the Ottoman Empire, suddenly found itself powerless, and many Sunnis feared domination by the Shiite majority. Many went underground and began a largely decentralized insurgency against their Shiite enemies. Many former Ba'athist leaders and party members joined, bringing arms and military experience with them.

Although some Shiite leaders, such as Grand Ayatollah Ali al-Sistani, called for calm, others were all too eager to take up arms against the Sunnis. Firebrand Shiite leader Moqtada al-Sadr, the son of a popular cleric who was killed after criticizing the Saddam Hussein government, led the Mahdi Army against the Sunnis and the American occupiers. Death squads connected to the Mahdi Army regularly captured and summarily killed ordinary Sunni citizens.

There was also a huge amount of resentment among both Sunnis and Shiites against the American occupiers. Insurgents from both groups began to target American troops almost from the day they entered Baghdad. Eventually, more American soldiers were killed by the insurgency than during the invasion.

Some administration officials suspected that Saddam Hussein might be behind the insurgency, but after US forces captured him on December 13, 2003, nothing changed; the insurgency, and the violence, continued to grow. (Saddam was eventually tried by an Iraqi court for crimes against humanity, and he was executed by hanging on December 30, 2006.) Attacks increased from fewer than ten a day in May to more than thirty by the end of November 2003.[14] In 2004, insurgent attacks increased from an average of about 25 per day in January to over 60 per day by the end of the year. The largest one-day number was 150, during the Muslim holy month of Ramadan.[15] By the time George W. Bush left office, some 106,000 Iraqi civilians had died in the violence, according to iraqbodycount.org.

Insurgents used a variety of weapons, including surface to air missiles, rocket propelled grenades (RPGs), suicide bombers, and snipers. But their most feared weapon soon became the improvised explosive device (IED). First used against American troops in Afghanistan, IEDs were easy to fabricate and conceal, and thus impossible to defend against. The bomber could plant the device by the roadside, and detonate it when soldiers passed. By the end of 2007, approximately 64% of Coalition fatalities resulted from IED attacks.[16]

The US military conducted several operations during the summer of 2003 that attempted to suppress the insurgency. Unfortunately, these raids were often heavy-handed and indiscriminate, resulting in more resentment from all Iraqis. The insurgency continued to worsen.

On March 31, 2004, opposition fighters in the city of Fallujah ambushed a convoy of American military contractors, killing four. Their bodies were dragged through the streets, burned, and then hung over a bridge across the Euphrates River. The American public was outraged at this display of barbarism. US forces commenced operations in Fallujah on April 4th, after surrounding the city with thousands of troops. As many as one-third of the civilian residents fled the city. But even with air support, the Americans were not able to dislodge the insurgents. By the time US troops withdrew from Fallujah on May 1st, 27 American soldiers had been killed, along with about 800 Iraqis, most of whom were civilians. Insurgents remained in control of the city.

Meanwhile, Moqtada al Sadr's Mahdi Army began a number of assaults in which they seized control of Najaf, a Shiite holy city, as well as other areas in the south of Iraq. US Marines attacked the Mahdi Army after an assault on a police station in Najaf; after three weeks of combat, the Mahdi Army was reduced to a few hundred fighters defending the Imam Ali shrine. A ceasefire agreement brokered by Grand Ayatollah al-Sistani called for both the Mahdi Army and the Marines to withdraw from the city. Both parties complied, but the Mahdi Army remained a player in the insurgency, continuing to control the Sadr City slums in Baghdad.

Another, larger attempt to retake Fallujah began on November 7, 2004, employing six battalions of Army, Marine, and Iraqi forces. Although pockets of resistance persisted for months, the Coalition troops had largely pacified the city by November 15th. Described as the largest battle fought by US forces since the Vietnam War, the second Battle of Fallujah resulted in 95 Americans killed and another 560 wounded. Estimates of insurgent deaths range from 1200 to 2000.[17]

The Bush administration considered this battle a victory, but insurgent attacks continued, in Fallujah and elsewhere in Iraq.

There was a lull in the violence during most of early 2005, including during and just after the national elections that were held at the end of January. Insurgent attacks declined from an average of 70 per day to around 30.

But attacks on Shiite civilians increased dramatically in May, making it the bloodiest month in Iraq since the US invasion began. In February of 2006, insurgents bombed the Askariya

Mosque, one of Shia Islam's holiest shrines. In retaliation, Shiite militias, including al-Sadr's Mahdi Army, attacked several Sunni mosques in Baghdad. Thousands rioted. As a result of such incidents, the insurgency became more and more sectarian in the following months, leading many military officials to start describing the violence as a civil war, rather than an insurgency. The Bush administration was loath to call it such; fighting an insurgency is one thing, but being stuck in the middle of a civil war would be about the worst outcome the Bush Administration could have hoped for. A report to Secretary of State Condoleezza Rice called Iraq a "failed state."[18]

The Surge

After more than three years of conflict in Iraq, the situation began to cost the Bush Administration support among both government leaders and the American people in general. The Democratic Party took control of both houses of the Congress in the mid-term elections of 2006; many pundits stated that the election was a referendum on the war in Iraq. Voices calling for the US to get out of Iraq became louder and more strident.

Meanwhile, studies by various groups, including the National Defense University, The American Enterprise Institute, and the Iraq Study Group suggested that an increase in US troops in Iraq could help stem the violence and provide some measure of stability. In December, President Bush met with experts on Iraq and with the Joint Chiefs of Staff to discuss their options. Although there was disagreement among military leaders about the efficacy of a bigger military presence, Bush decided to go that route. In January 2007, Bush announced what he called "The New Way Forward." In a televised speech, he declared, "I've committed more than 20,000 additional American troops to Iraq."[19] In addition, Bush extended the tour of most Army and Marine personnel already in the country.

Surge operations began in February with a plan to secure Baghdad, although it was not until June that full troop deployment allowed counter-insurgency efforts to fully get underway. That same month, US troops began operations against insurgents in Diyala and Anbar provinces, as well as other areas.

Along with the troop buildup, anti-insurgency tactics began to change under the new commander in Iraq, General David Petraeus. His strategy was to focus on protecting civilians, rather than hunting down insurgents. Petraeus also worked on building trust with Iraqi communities, hoping to gain local cooperation in improving security in the country.

Although violence increased at the beginning of the surge, the security situation gradually improved. US military deaths decreased from a high of 126 in May 2007, to 23 in December. Iraqi civilian deaths also decreased significantly in 2007.[20] While Petraeus declared that the surge was responsible for the improving situation, the surge also coincided with Moqtada al-Sadr's cease-fire order to his Mahdi Army. US General James Jones suggested that violence had subsided because Sunni or Shiite partisans had pacified some areas by overrunning them. What ever the main cause, by July of 2008 US troop casualties were at their lowest point since the invasion began in 2003. Credit, however, is also due also to the movement known as the Sunni Awakening.

Sunni Awakening

Anbar Province in western Iraq is majority Sunni, and when al-Qaida in Iraq took control of the province, local sheiks cooperated with it in opposing the Shiite-led government. However, the sheiks soon became horrified by al-Qaida's brutality. They therefore allied themselves with American and Iraqi troops in order to push al-Qaida out of Anbar Province. With training and money from the US military, this *ad hoc* coalition eventually succeeded in driving al-Qaida from Ramadi and Fallujah, the two largest cities in Anbar. Al-Qaida, however, was still active in Iraq, although some suggested that they softened their tactics in response to the Sunni Awakening.[21]

24

Although it is certain that the Sunni Awakening helped to quell the sectarian violence and to integrate some Sunnis back into the mainstream, there were conflicts with the Iraqi government, including a two-day battle with government forces over the arrest of an Awakening leader on murder charges. Insurgent groups systematically targeted Awakening leaders and members in Anbar Province.

Iraqi government leaders were not comfortable with a fighting force that was not under their control, and worked hard to disband the tribal coalition. In October of 2008, the Iraqi government began paying the Awakening fighters, and by June 2012 some 70,000 members had been absorbed into the Iraq defense forces or given civilian jobs.

Drawdown of US Troops

Right after the fall of Baghdad, Defense Secretary Donald Rumsfeld planned to reduce US troops in Iraq to some 40,000 by the autumn of 2003. But when the Iraqis failed to welcome us as liberators, and began to fight amongst themselves and against American forces instead, that original plan had to be scrapped. In fact, as we have seen, American leaders had found it necessary to increase the US troop presence in an effort to quell the burgeoning violence.

But as the fighting worsened, and the war dragged on, more and more voices began calling for the US to begin withdrawing from Iraq. Many Iraqis, of course, had been calling for the US to get out from the beginning, but support in the United States began to soften also as more and more Americans were killed fighting the insurgency. Once the Democrats took control of Congress in January 2007, Party leaders began to push for troop withdrawals. Congressional Democrats passed a bill ordering troops to begin withdrawing in 2007, but President Bush vetoed the bill, while publicly denouncing the legislation. "It makes no sense to tell the enemy when you plan to start withdrawing," he said.[22] Throughout the war, Bush adamantly opposed any talk of withdrawing before the job was completed.

He was unwavering in his conviction that we had to stay the course until we were victorious. (Under the circumstances, part of the problem was defining victory.) But by late 2007, military and civilian leaders, including George W. Bush, began talking about troop reductions. American units began a slow withdrawal in late 2007; by the end of the Bush presidency in December 2008, 146,000 American soldiers remained in Iraq, down from a high of approximately 162,000 in August of 2007.

In 2008, the Iraqi government and the Bush Administration signed a Status of Forces agreement stating that American troops would withdraw from Iraqi cities by June 30, 2009, and from the country entirely by December 31, 2011. Bush, having failed to achieve victory, left it to his successor, Democrat Barack Obama, to finish the war in Iraq.

Due to the situation on the ground, Obama extended the date of withdrawal from Iraqi cities from June 30, 2009, to August 31, 2010, while committing to the 2011 date for complete withdrawal. On August 19, 2010, the last US combat forces left Iraq, more than seven years after the invasion. Some 50,000 troops remained in the country, mostly in a training and advisory capacity.

When it became apparent that the fighting in Iraq, whether one called it an insurgency or a civil war, was not going to end by December 2011, the Obama Administration attempted to renegotiate the Status of Forces agreement. The US government wanted Iraq to provide immunity to American troops from prosecution by Iraqi courts for any alleged crimes. The Iraqi government would not agree to this, and the American government was not going to leave forces in the country without such an agreement, so the original withdrawal timetable was kept. On December 15, 2011, a ceremony in Baghdad marked the official end to the US military presence in Iraq. The last 500 American soldiers left Iraq on that same day. At the time, more than 4,400 Americans had lost their lives in the conflict.

Iraq Today

The departure of US troops did not bring peace to Iraq. Sectarian conflict continued, even worsened, while the elected Iraqi government remained weak, divided and unable to control the country. According to Iraq Body Count, nearly 10,800 Iraqis have been killed in the violence since the US withdrawal in December 2011.[23]

National elections in 2014 failed to give any one party a clear majority, and national leaders could not cobble together a coalition to rule the country. Prime minister Nouri al-Malaki, seen as too pro-Shiite, faced mounting pressure to resign, both at home and from the US government, and he finally did in August 2014. The Iraqi president appointed Haider al-Abadi, a former Shiite exile under the Saddam Hussein regime, as the new prime minister. Abadi was at first unable to form a government due to opposition from al-Malaki, but he finally succeeded after al-Malaki dropped his protests. Abadi has since worked, with limited success, to stem corruption in the military and police, bring more Sunnis into the government, and improve relations with neighboring nations.

In December 2010 anti-government riots erupted in the North African nation of Tunisia after a street vendor named Mohamed Bouazizi set himself on fire in protest over corruption and his treatment by local officials. The protests led to a popular uprising, which in turn led to the overthrow of the Tunisian regime; President Zine Ben Ali fled into exile. By 2014, Tunisia had released political prisoners, abolished the former ruling political party, and formed a new, parliamentary government.

The success of the Tunisian revolution encouraged people living under other repressive regimes in the Arab world to start their own protests. The results were not the same as in Tunisia, however. In Libya, rebels overthrew and brutally murdered dictator Muammar Gaddafi. However, another repressive government took power. This government was overthrown with help from the US and European militaries, but Libya remains a failed state to this day.

A popular uprising in Egypt managed to drive long-time despot Hosni Mubarak from power. Elections were held, which were dominated by the formerly outlawed Muslim Brotherhood; the Brotherhood's Mohamed Morsi was elected president. However, just when it seemed that democracy had come to Egypt, Morsi was overthrown by the military, and a new president, a general, was installed, effectively ending popular rule in Egypt. The Muslim Brotherhood was again outlawed.

In Syria, a neighbor of Iraq, the so-called Arab Spring began with protests against the regime of President Bashar al-Assad, who has been in power since the death of his father, Hafez al-Assad, in 2000. Assad responded to the protests with a harsh, severe crackdown. The protesters began to call for Assad to resign, and the repression became even more Draconian; thousands were arrested and many protesters were killed. Several armed groups declared themselves in rebellion against the Assad regime in response to the heavy-handed attempts to suppress the uprising. Syria soon became engulfed in a bitter, multi-sided civil war that continues to this day.

The repercussions for Iraq have been nothing short of disastrous. A group led by jihadist Abu Musab al-Zarqawi, which came to be known commonly as al-Qaida in Iraq, was a participant in the insurgency fighting the US occupation. After merging with other jihadist groups in Iraq, the organization renamed itself the Islamic State of Iraq and Syria, or ISIS for short. Also known as the Islamic State of Iraq and the Levant, the group had been driven from Anbar Province by the Sunni Awakening in 2008.

The civil war in Syria created a power vacuum that ISIS took full advantage of. After capturing a significant amount of territory in Syria, ISIS established a self-styled capital in the eastern Syrian city of Raqqah and declared itself to be a worldwide Islamic caliphate. In 2014, ISIS fighters succeeded in capturing much of northern and western Iraq, including the cities of Fallujah and Ramadi, and 70% of Anbar province. Mosul, Iraq's third largest city, soon fell to ISIS also, in part due to Nouri al-Malaki's refusal to accept help from Kurdish Peshmerga fighters. ISIS also captured Tikrit, the hometown of Saddam Hussein, and Diyala province, putting ISIS uncomfortably close to Baghdad. Iraqi government forces were powerless to stop them. Indeed, many Iraqi soldiers fled the battlefield, shedding their uniforms as they ran.

Northern Iraq is majority Kurdish. The Kurds, whose territory extends from southeastern Turkey, across northern Syria and Iraq, and into northwestern Iran, are the largest stateless ethnic group in the world. But since the Gulf War of the early 1990s, Iraq's Kurds have enjoyed a large degree of autonomy. The Kurds have their own defense forces, called the Peshmerga, and they were instrumental in halting and eventually pushing back the advance of ISIS.

ISIS ruled its conquered territory with a level of brutality that was shocking even to other jihadist leaders. Beheadings and mass executions became common. ISIS destroyed ancient Mesopotamian artifacts and monuments, humanity's heritage of the earliest civilizations, because they were considered idolatrous. An especially harsh form of Sharia (Islamic law) was imposed on the citizens of occupied territory. Minorities such as the non-Muslim Yazidis were besieged and slaughtered in an alleged attempt at genocide. The Iraqi defense forces were powerless to stop ISIS. Iraq was in danger of devolving into a truly failed state, or worse perhaps, the center of the ISIS caliphate.

In response to the Yazidi imperilment, President Obama authorized airstrikes against the Islamic State in August of 2014, thus returning American forces to the conflict in Iraq. In August, American air strikes and Peshmerga troops broke the siege of Mt. Sinjar, where ISIS had trapped the Yazidis.

The fighting continued throughout 2014 and 2015; Iraqi defense forces or Kurdish Peshmerga would take back territory while ISIS would take some other territory. But by June of 2016, ISIS had been pushed out of both Fallujah and Ramadi, as well as all of Diyala province, northeast of Baghdad. Attempts to retake Mosul, however, have so far failed to completely drive ISIS out.

Meanwhile, the Sunni insurgency continues, ISIS continues to occupy large parts of Iraq, and the central government continues to be weak and ineffective. Iraq continues to be a divided, violent and poor country, despite vast oil reserves. A destabilizing civil war continues next door in Syria. It's going to be a long, long time until Iraq can even start to be a stable and prosperous country.

PART 2: THE CASE

The Charges

We charge the George Walker Bush Administration, in general, and President George W. Bush, Vice-President Richard Cheney, Secretary of Defense Donald Rumsfeld, Assistant Secretary of Defense Paul Wolfowitz, CIA Director George Tenet, and National Security Advisor Condoleezza Rice, in particular, with lying to the American public about the alleged threat that Iraqi dictator Saddam Hussein posed to the United States. They lied in order to convince the American people that we needed to invade Iraq because we faced imminent danger from Saddam. The truth is, the above named individuals entered office with a desire to "deal with" Saddam Hussein from day one, well before 9/11. Their neo-conservative dogma held that George Bush the elder should have deposed Saddam Hussein during the 1991 Gulf War to dislodge the Iraqi dictator from the neighboring state of Kuwait. The neo-cons felt George H.W. Bush did not finish the job, and the new Bush administration should and would.

The only problem was to convince the American people to go along with this scheme, but how? Bush and company would have had a hard time convincing the country to go along with an invasion of Iraq by claiming that Saddam was a bad guy and he had to go. There are plenty of bad actors on the world stage, but it should not be the responsibility of the US military to rid other

31

nations of their dictators. The Bush Administration needed a more compelling reason to convince the American people to go along with an unprovoked invasion.

Then, out of the blue, America was attacked by al-Qaida operatives on September 11, 2001, an attack that killed approximately 3,000 people, destroyed billions of dollars worth of property, and created a near irrational fear of terrorism among the American populace.

The Bush Administration suddenly had a compelling reason for an invasion, even if it was based on lies: terrorism. The Administration cynically decided to take advantage of America's fear of terrorism to convince the people that Saddam Hussein was part of the terrorist threat that we faced.

What the Administration Said

The following statements were made by Administration officials claiming that Saddam Hussein's Iraq posed an imminent threat to the United States, and thus had to be attacked before he, or terrorist surrogates, could attack us.

"Simply stated, there is no doubt that Saddam Hussein now has weapons of mass destruction. There is no doubt that he is amassing them to use against us."
–Vice President Richard Cheney[24]

"We know for a fact that there are weapons there."
–Press secretary Ari Fleischer[25]

"We know [Saddam Hussein] has reconstituted these [chemical weapons] programs. We know he's out trying once again to produce nuclear weapons, and we know that he has a long-standing relationship with various terrorist groups, including the al-Qaida organization."
–Vice President Cheney[26]

"Iraq has at least seven mobile factories for the production of biological agents. Iraq could produce within just months hundreds of pounds of biological poisons."

–President George W. Bush[27]

"[Iraq] possesses and produces chemical and biological weapons. It is seeking nuclear weapons."

–President George W. Bush[28]

"We know that Iraq has at least seven of these mobile biological agent factories. They can produce enough dry biological agent in a single month to kill thousands upon thousands of people."

–Secretary of State Colin Powell[29]

"The British government has learned that Saddam Hussein recently sought significant quantities of uranium from Africa. Our intelligence sources tell us that he has attempted to purchase high-strength aluminum tubes suitable for nuclear weapons."

–President George W. Bush[30]

"If we know Saddam Hussein has dangerous weapons today–and we do..."

–President George W. Bush[31]

"Saddam Hussein still has chemical and biological weapons and is increasing his capabilities to make more."

–President George W. Bush[32]

"We know they have weapons of mass destruction. We know they have active programs. There isn't any debate about it."[33]

–Secretary of Defense Donald Rumsfeld.

"It's been pretty well confirmed that (Atta) did go to Prague, and he did meet with a senior official of the Iraqi intelligence service in (the Czech Republic) last April, several months before the attack."

–Vice President Richard Cheney[34]

"We know that Iraq and al-Qaida have had high-level contacts that go back a decade."

–President George W. Bush[35]

And the list goes on and on; we could cite many other such statements made by Administration officials in the run-up to the invasion of Iraq, but this list should be sufficient evidence for our purposes here.

In all these statements, made in public to promote the administration's case for war, the speaker states his assertions as fact: "there is no doubt," "we know for a fact," "Iraq has." In the case of Bush's comments about uranium, he was citing intelligence that he had already been warned was unreliable (more on that below).

This is the crux of the case for war crimes and the assertion that the Bush Administration lied; they said they *knew* Saddam had weapons of mass destruction (WMD). In fact they did *not* know; they *could* not know that Saddam had WMD, because he in fact did *not* possess WMD, as became clear in the months and years after the invasion of Iraq. If Bush and allies had said we *believe* Saddam has WMD, there would be no case for war crimes. (There may never have been a war, for that matter.) But Bush, Cheney, et al. said they *knew* the Iraqi dictator had these weapons, when they actually knew no such thing.

We intend to prove that the above statements, as well as others, were lies that the Bush Administration told in order sell the American public on a war against a country that was not threatening the United States, or its neighbors, and which had nothing to do with the 9/11 terrorist attacks in the United States.

We will show that Bush, Cheney, and Rumsfeld, among others, wanted to take action against Saddam Hussein from the day they took office, and that they plotted how they might accomplish this, until 9/11 gave them their opportunity.

If the invasion of Iraq was not about WMD, or alleged terrorist connections, then what was it about? We will address this question in the section titled "Motivation." But first, let us address our allegations that the George W. Bush Administration entered office with a desire to destroy the regime of Saddam Hussein.

Bringing Down Saddam

In 1998, a group of Republican Party leaders wrote a letter to then-President Bill Clinton urging him to take action against Saddam Hussein. This document, written as an open letter to the President, made the same claims that the George W. Bush Administration would lay out as its reasons for invading Iraq five years later. The letter claimed that despite sanctions, "Saddam Hussein has been able to develop biological and chemical munitions." The authors asserted that Saddam was likely to use these weapons, not just against his neighbors, but against the US and its allies as well. "What is needed now is a comprehensive political and military strategy for bringing down Saddam and his regime," the letter said.[36] This letter stated that taking action against Saddam Hussein's Iraq was in the national interest of the United States. It stated categorically that we, the Unites States, needed to effect regime change in Iraq. This missive was signed by, among others, Donald Rumsfeld, Paul Wolfowitz, and Douglas Feith. In the George W. Bush Administration, these three men would head the Defense Department, and would be among the leading proponents for a pre-emptive war against Saddam Hussein. The letter was also signed by others who would become significant players in the Bush Administration and its policy of regime change in Iraq.

The signatories to this letter formed the core of the neo-conservative movement that believed that the United States needed to be more forceful in its foreign policy, in order to make the world safe for democracy (as well as for American foreign policy objectives).

In January of 2001, ten days into his administration, George Bush held a meeting of the principle members of his National Security Council. This meeting included Secretary of Defense Donald Rumsfeld, Vice-President Richard Cheney, National Security advisor Condoleezza Rice, and Secretary of State Colin Powell. After Bush declared that the United States would no longer attempt to broker a peace agreement between Israel and the Palestinians, the subject turned to Iraq. The topic was broached when Rice declared that "Iraq is destabilizing the area [the Middle East]." Upon which CIA Director George Tenet dragged out grainy aerial surveillance photos of a factory in Iraq that the CIA believed was producing either chemical or biological weapons. When questioned by Treasury Secretary Paul O'Neill, Tenet admitted there was "no confirming evidence."[37] In fact, Tenet stated that intelligence on Saddam's weapons programs was very poor. Nonetheless, the meeting concluded with a number of action items on Iraq. Powell would look into strengthening the sanctions regime, while Rumsfeld would "examine our military options."

Early in 2001, Cheney and Rumsfeld started circulating memos with names like "Plan for Post-Saddam Iraq" and "Foreign Suitors for Iraqi Oilfield Contracts." [38] This was obviously an administration that was heavily focused on Iraq and the elimination of Saddam Hussein, although they gave little public indication of their ambitions.

"From the start, we were building the case against Hussein and looking at how we could take him out," Treasury Secretary O'Neill said. "It was all about finding a way to do it."[39]

After 9/11, administration officials pushed even harder for an invasion of Iraq. Just hours after the attacks, Donald Rumsfeld met with senior military leaders to discuss the possibility of "hitting" Saddam Hussein, as well as Osama bin Laden. [40] Assistant Secretary of Defense Paul Wolfowitz (one of the authors of the above-mentioned letter to President Clinton) argued that al-Qaida could not have pulled off 9/11 without help from a state actor. Wolfowitz, not surprisingly, pointed to Iraq as the likely culprit. Rumsfeld began talking about "getting Iraq."[41]

At a National Security Council meeting on September 12, 2001–one day after the terrorist attacks–Rumsfeld brought up Iraq. He claimed that at some point, the war on terror would lead to Iraq. At a September 15th meeting at Camp David, the presidential retreat in the Maryland countryside, Wolfowitz again brought up Iraq, arguing that a war in Afghanistan would be a mess, but that Iraq was "doable." Bush got so tired of the attention given Iraq that he actually told Wolfowitz and others that he did not want to hear any more about Iraq that day.

In 2002 Wolfowitz and Douglas Feith created the Office of Special Plans (a rather vague, sinister-sounding moniker) within the Defense Department when the CIA, among others, was not providing any actionable intelligence on Iraqi weapons programs. The office was set up specifically to supply the Administration with intelligence on Iraq. OSP was responsible for digging up any evidence that Saddam had what the Administration was hoping to find: WMD, ties to al-Qaida, possibly even nuclear weapons.[42]

Given all this evidence, it is clear that the Bush Administration wanted to go to war with Iraq, not just before 9/11, but before Bush and company were even in office. All they were waiting for was an opportunity.

Attempts to Provoke a Fight with Iraq

After the 1991 Gulf War, the United States and its allies enforced so-called no-fly zones in Iraq. Sanctioned by the United Nations, these no-fly zones were designed to protect Shite Arabs in southern Iraq and the Kurdish population in northern Iraq. Both groups had been targets of oppression by the Hussein regime. When George Bush came into office, tactics shifted to selecting military command structures as targets. Attacks on such targets were designed to weaken Iraqi defenses in the event of any invasion by American or allied forces. The Bush administration also hoped that such action could provoke Saddam to retaliate, thus giving the US a reason to invade Iraq.

The Administration commenced what they called Operation Southern Focus in June of 2002. Without any public announcement, this operation dramatically increased bombing of selected targets being conducted as part of the enforcement of the no-fly zones. By September, bombing increased to 54 tons of ordinance in strikes by as many as 100 aircraft.[43] These strikes were conducted to destroy air defense and command and control installations ahead of an invasion, while also trying to provoke a response from Saddam Hussein. If Saddam reacted militarily to the bombing, the Administration would have its excuse to invade Iraq. All of this occurred well before the US Congress authorized Bush to use the military against Iraq in October of 2002.

In a meeting with British Prime Minister Tony Blair in January of 2003, George Bush reportedly discussed ways of provoking a fight with Iraq, including painting a U-2 spy plane with United Nations colors and flying it low over Iraq, in the hope that Saddam would shoot it down. Bush informed Blair that he had already decided to invade Iraq, stating, "The start date for the military campaign was penciled in for 10 March." At this meeting, Bush and Blair agreed that the war against Iraq would proceed whether or not UN inspectors found any WMD.[44]

Propaganda Machine

"All you have to do is tell [the people] that they are being attacked and denounce the pacifists for lack of patriotism and exposing the country to danger. It works the same way in any country." –Hermann Goering, Nazi leader

The word propaganda comes from a Latin word meaning to propagate, as in to spread something such as a seed, or an idea–like as a desire to go to war. According to Webster, propaganda is any systematic, widespread, deliberate indoctrination or plan for indoctrination. Another, simpler way to describe propaganda is to equate it with rhetoric: speech that is designed to convince you of the speaker's point of view, or to buy what the speaker is selling. The Bush Administration needed to use just such language to sell America on starting another war–as we were already prosecuting a war in Afghanistan.

Once the Bush Administration decided to invade Iraq and depose Saddam Hussein, it had to convince the American public to go along, if for no other reason than to convince Congress to give its approval. If the Administration could create enough fear that we were imminently facing another 9/11, public reaction could compel the Congress to give Bush permission to move against Saddam militarily. Cynically capitalizing on the fear engendered in the country following the 9/11 attacks, Bush cranked up the propaganda machine and set the administration to work selling an invasion to the American public.

To exploit America's fear of terrorism, Bush and company had to link Iraq and Saddam Hussein to terrorists, and make that connection repeatedly in order to get the message to sink into the minds of the American people. For example, in a speech in Cincinnati, Ohio, in October, 2002, Bush repeatedly intimated or stated outright that Saddam Hussein was connected with international terrorists, even stating that "Iraq and al-Qaida have had high-level contacts that go back a decade,"[45] an assertion that had no basis in fact.

In 2004, well after the invasion, the House Committee on Government Reform published a report entitled Iraq on the Record. This report states that five people, Bush, Cheney, Rumsfeld, Powell, and Rice, had made a total of "237 misleading statements about the threat posed by Iraq." The statements were drawn from 125 speeches or appearances made between March 2002 and January of 2004. The biggest monthly total during that time was the 30 days just prior to the congressional vote to authorize the President to use force against Iraq. That is, the Administration stepped up the propaganda campaign in order to pressure the Congress to allow the use of force against Iraq. The 237 statements claimed that Iraq posed an imminent threat, that Saddam had or was developing WMD, including nuclear weapons, and that Iraq had ties to al Qaida. (Investigators determined what was misleading by comparing what the officials said with what the intelligence actually showed at the time the statements were made.)[46]

Former Bush press secretary Scott McClellan released a book in 2008 in which he criticized the Administration for waging a "political propaganda campaign." McClellan states, "He [Bush] set the policy early on and then his team focused their attention on how to sell it," and that Bush was not "open and forthright on Iraq." McClellan goes so far as to suggest that Bush "sometimes...convinces himself to believe what suits his needs at the moment."[47] And this is exactly how he approached his efforts to sell the war; he attempted to convince Americans to believe what he needed them to believe, whether it was true or not.

The Administration went so far as to create a public relations campaign for a "PR blitz against Saddam Hussein," according to the *Times* of London. This campaign would employ the same techniques as advertisers to convince their targeted audiences that "the Iraqi leader must be ousted."[48]

As any good propagandist knows, if you repeat something often enough, people will begin to believe it, even if it is a lie. And so, Bush trotted out all the Administration heavyweights to all the news and talk shows and other media outlets, to bang the drum for a war with Iraq. In speeches and interviews, Bush, Cheney, Rumsfeld, Condoleezza Rice, Colin Powell and others avowed repeatedly that Saddam Hussein posed an imminent threat to the United States and that he must be eliminated before it was too late. They were, again, preying on the fear Americans were gripped with after 9/11.

Pre-Invasion Actions and Troop Movements

Even before Congress had authorized the Bush Administration to use force against Iraq in October 2002, operations against Saddam Hussein were already underway. In July of 2002, the CIA inserted into Iraq what were known as Special Activities Division teams.[49] These paramilitary teams participated, along with Army Special Forces, in a battle against Ansar al-Islam, a terrorist group operating in Iraq (but not affiliated with Saddam Hussein). That is, US forces were already engaging in combat in Iraq before Congress gave the authorization to use force against Saddam. The CIA teams also worked to identify leaders to be targeted during the invasion, an invasion that had yet to be sanctioned by the US Congress.

As stated in the brief history of the war, the United Nations refused to authorize an invasion of Iraq, opting instead to resume weapons inspections, a proposal that Saddam Hussein agreed to in November of 2002. In February of 2003, United Nations and International Atomic Energy Agency inspectors reported that they found "no evidence or plausible indication" of a revival of Iraqi weapons programs. The UN report stated that inspectors "did not find evidence of the continuation or resumption of programs of weapons of mass destruction or significant quantities of proscribed items."[50]

But the Bush Administration wasn't going to wait for the UN inspections process to run its course. In December of 2002, President Bush authorized the deployment of approximately 200,000 American troops to the Middle East. Because it is so expensive to move troops and equipment, once that juggernaut has been set in motion, it is almost impossible to stop. Deployment means that the troops *are going to be used*. Bush and company were going to invade Iraq, regardless of what any United Nations weapons inspectors might have to say.

Weapons of Mass Destruction

"For bureaucratic reasons, we settled on one issue—weapons of mass destruction—because it was the one reason everyone could agree on." –Paul Wolfowitz[51]

The intelligence community did not come to the Bush Administration with warnings about Iraq, which the Administration then acted on. Rather, Bush and company made claims about Iraq and then went to the intelligence community and bade them to find evidence for their claims. Or as former CIA Intelligence Officer Paul Pillar put it, "Intelligence was misused publicly to justify decisions that had already been made."[52]

This point cannot be stressed enough; this was not a case of taking action based on good intelligence; rather, it was a case of making accusations and then looking for evidence to back up the claims.

Vice President Dick Cheney began hounding the CIA to find evidence regarding any Iraqi WMD programs. Cheney's repeated visits to CIA headquarters prompted the House Intelligence Committee to send a letter to the Vice President rebuking him for his efforts.[53] When the CIA did not come up with anything the Administration could use, Paul Wolfowitz and Douglas Feith set up the aforementioned Office of Special Plans specifically to dig for any evidence to support the Administration's claims. The Pentagon also established the Counter Terrorism Evaluation Unit, and it also was tasked with cherry-picking the intelligence to find evidence of WMD in Iraq.[54]

As noted above, Bush, Cheney, et al. repeatedly asserted that Saddam Hussein was amassing weapons of mass destruction, and that Saddam intended to use them against the United States. Weapons of mass destruction can include anything from chemical or biological weapons to nuclear bombs; the Bush Administration claimed or intimated that Saddam either had all of them or was developing them. They claimed that Iraq had mobile biological weapons factories, that Iraq was attempting to obtain uranium ore for nuclear weapons, and that it had purchased aluminum tubes for use in producing nuclear weapons.

We will debunk each of these claims in turn. As we examine them, it would be instructive to remember that CIA Director George Tenet, in the first national security team meeting of the Bush Administration, had admitted that US intelligence on Iraq's weapons programs was very poor (see Bringing Down Saddam, above).

MOBILE BIOLOGICAL WEAPONS FACTORIES

The Administration's assertions regarding Saddam's attempts to produce biological weapons were based almost entirely on the "intelligence" gleaned from an informant that no American intelligence personnel ever interviewed. He was a German intelligence source who was known by the code name

Curveball. Unless otherwise noted, the following reporting regarding this informant comes from a book of the same name, by Pulitzer Prize winning journalist Bob Drogin.[55]

Ahmed Hassan Mohammed (an assumed name) was an Iraqi defector who fled to Germany in 1999. When his plane landed in Munich, Mohammed asked for political asylum. Customs officials interviewed him at the airport; they subsequently sent Mohammed to a refuge center in Nuremburg. As was customary, agents of Germany's Federal Intelligence Service (BND) interviewed Mohammed there. He told the BND that he had worked as a chemical engineer at the Iraqi Chemical Engineering and Design Center in the late 1990s, and that he had worked on a program to construct mobile biological weapons factories.

Eventually code-named Curveball by the Americans, Mohammed fed his German interrogators this information in bits and pieces, tantalizing them with these tidbits, while leveraging his position to get himself better living conditions, some cash and other amenities, all provided by the BND. Curveball, over time, named names, companies and commissions; he described technical details of equipment and processes. Curveball's descriptions of the process of producing bioweapons were accurate, according to experts in the field.

Curveball also described the alleged mobile bio-weapons factory that was cited by the Administration as proof of Saddam's plans, most notably by Secretary of State Colin Powell in a speech to the United Nations. The design, according to Curveball, included three truck trailers containing fermenters for incubating the biological agents, such as anthrax. The trailers also included mixing and storage tanks and spray dryers, as drying the toxins give them a longer shelf life.

He also claimed to have worked on these mobile factories at a facility southeast of Baghdad called Djerf al Nadaf. He said the trailers were built there, and that the site would also act as a docking station for loading and unloading materials. His descriptions of this warehouse were very detailed; he described an oddly shaped building that the large trucks pulling the bioweapons trailers would have to pull through, as there was not room enough to turn around. So, according to Curveball, they built a swinging door right into one corner of the building, a hinged corner of sorts. He also stated that biological materials were stored in a hidden underground chamber. These details would eventually help to expose Curveball as a fraud, as we shall see.

The BND sent copies of its reports on Curveball to other agencies, including the US Defense Intelligence Agency (DIA). DIA arranged to interview Curveball in the spring of 2000, but its agents were denied access to the informant. Curveball's German handler told the DIA agents that Curveball hated Americans and refused to talk to them, but the truth is that the Germans were reluctant to share their asset, in part because they didn't want to share information that could put Germany in a bad light. Curveball had claimed that the germ factories were constructed in part with German-built components. Germany had already suffered a scandal over reports that German companies had sold plans and materials for bioweapons to both Libya and Iraq, and the BND did not want to be the source of another, similar scandal. What's more, there had been bad blood between the BND and the American intelligence agencies for years, and they didn't always cooperate.

When the BND sent its reports to the DIA, they included the caveat that the reliability of the information "cannot be verified." DIA's versions of these reports said simply that the accuracy of the report could not be determined, which may seem to say the same thing, but the designation meant that DIA was willing to give the report more weight, or to "sex it up," in intelligence community jargon. This became a trend with ensuing Curveball reports. By the summer of 2000, American intelligence agencies became very interested in Curveball, even though the Germans continued to deny American agents the opportunity to interview him.

But his story began to unravel. He claimed to have been accidentally exposed to anthrax, an accident that Curveball claimed killed several workers. If so, there should have been traces of anthrax in his blood, but none were found. Investigators discovered that most of the names and agencies he cited were readily available on the Internet. He became irritable, evasive and uncooperative. He began to contradict himself, refuting details he had provided in earlier interviews, even saying that he had not worked on the bioweapons trailers, but had only heard about them from other people. "He is saying one thing in the morning and another at night," complained one of his German handlers.

In March of 2001, the BND warned the CIA that Curveball had changed some of his stories, and that his story was "presently compromised by reporting inconsistencies."

Eventually, American intelligence agents were able to check on Curveball's story. They obtained his official Iraqi government employee records, which showed that Curveball was a problem employee, and that he had been fired by the government in 1995. Curveball was not working on any bioweapons factories in the late 1990s, as he had claimed. He claimed he witnessed the deadly accident in 1998, but he was not there in 1998. The CIA located and talked to his mother; she told them that he travelled abroad extensively between 1995 and 1998. She also told the agents that her son actually loved Americans, something that didn't sit well with the CIA. Due in part to these revelations, the BND terminated their interrogation of Curveball in September of 2001. That same month, BND agents told the CIA that they couldn't verify Curveball's stories because they had no other sources, and that his handlers believed that he was "a fabricator." They still would not allow the CIA to interview Curveball.

Despite all the uncertainty surrounding Curveball's assertions, the Bush Administration was eager to use this intelligence in its war propaganda. Bush wanted to use Curveball in his 2003 State of the Union speech. The CIA was alarmed at this prospect, because they knew the information was unconfirmed. So the CIA again asked the BND for access to Curveball, or at least, transcripts of BND's interviews with him. When the BND again refused these requests, the CIA agent handling the case told the CIA deputy director, who regularly briefed the President, that the Curveball intelligence could not be validated or corroborated. Nonetheless, when Bush appeared before the Congress for his speech, he declared, "...we know that Iraq had several mobile weapons labs...he's given no evidence that he has destroyed them."[56] Of course Saddam gave no such evidence; you can't destroy something you never built.

American intelligence agents, as well as the Germans, were shocked that Bush had used the Curveball story, and continued to warn the White House that this intelligence was "soft." Yet Bush again cited the Curveball story in a radio speech and White House statement: "Firsthand witnesses have informed us that Iraq has at least seven mobile weapons factories for the production of biological agents. Iraq could produce within just months hundreds of pounds of biological poisons."

Vice President Dick Cheney did not mention Curveball by name, but in a speech to a veteran's convention in Nashville, in which Cheney stated, "there is no doubt that Saddam...has weapons of mass destruction," he also said, "we often learned more as the result of defections." Cheney made this speech without first clearing it with the CIA, which was standard practice for speeches referring to intelligence gathered by American agencies.

Before Secretary of State Colin Powell's speech to the United Nations in February of 2003, he huddled with CIA Director George Tenet. Tenet reassured Powell that the intelligence on mobile weapons factories was "totally reliable information," even though his staff had already told him "there are problems with the German case." A DIA official who was present at this meeting was aware that his own agency had issued a fabrication notice regarding Curveball, but he said nothing to Secretary Powell. So Powell can perhaps be forgiven for presenting the mobile weapons factory story to the UN, because the intelligence services had not been honest with him.

However, the CIA chief and the DIA officer, along with the intelligence community in general, were under pressure from Bush and Cheney to exploit whatever intelligence they had, whether it could be corroborated or not. This is indicative of an administration that was determined to go to war with Iraq, and that it was desperately grasping at any intelligence that would bolster their case. "This war is going to happen regardless of what Curveball said or didn't say, and the Powers That Be probably aren't terribly interested in whether Curveball knows what he's talking about," according to an Iraq WMD task force member. The Administration was going to run with the intelligence it had, whether it was good or not.

After the invasion, the Administration sent former UN weapons inspector David Kay back to Iraq to look for the elusive WMD. Kay had worked for the International Atomic Energy Agency, looking for WMD in Iraq after the 1991 Gulf War, and at first, he was sure that Iraq still had them, as were most of his staff. He would soon change his mind. He started by talking to the bioweapons team of the Iraq Survey Group. They told Kay that Curveball's story was "credible," a word that gave Kay a sick feeling, because he knew this was spy-speak that meant the information had not been validated. He asked about corroborating informants, and the agents admitted there weren't any.

Meanwhile, the bio-weapons team made six separate inspections of the supposed WMD processing site at Djerf al Nadaf that Curveball had described in great detail. It was not at all like he had reported. The CIA inspectors found no corner door, and that a large concrete wall outside the building stood in the way of any such door opening. Satellite images showed that this wall had been there since 1997; Curveball had claimed to work at Djerf al Nadaf at that time. The inspectors also looked for any other evidence of biological weapons production, but found none, not even traces of DNA. Inspectors went so far as to use ground-penetrating radar to look for the underground storage room; none was found. Curveball had fabricated his description of the facilities at Djerf al Nadaf.

Searches of other suspected sites also turned up nothing.

Two months after the fall of Baghdad, George Bush announced, "We have found the weapons of mass destruction." The inspectors did find truck trailers like those described by Curveball, but they turned out to be "singularly inappropriate" for producing bioweapons, and Bush new it. Analysis by Defense Intelligence Agency engineers and scientists had already determined that the trailers were not bioweapons factories; they filed their report two days before Bush made his declaration. The DIA's report was conveniently classified and shelved.[57]

A 2004 report by the Iraq Survey Group concluded that the trailers were almost certainly designed for "manufacturing hydrogen for weather balloons." The Group reported that these trailers lacked eleven essential components for bioweapons production. The team also noted that the trailers could not be easily modified for weapons production, saying, "It would be easier to start over." Other analysts pointed out that these trailers were not equipped with a containment system, meaning any road accidents could be very deadly and would expose Iraq's bioweapons program to the world.

Searchers also managed to turn up a handful of outdated, degraded chemical munitions that were left over from the Iran-Iraq War of the 1980s. A few politicians claimed that we had found the WMD that we had been looking for, but the shells were no longer useful as weapons. Charles Duelfer, David Kay's successor at the Iraq Survey Group, described the rounds as hazardous but not deadly. "They are not a major weapon of mass destruction," Duelfer told NPR's *Talk of the Nation*.[58]

These were the WMD that we went to war over.

On October 2, 2003, the CIA released a report written by Kay that stated he had found no anthrax, no smallpox, no biological weapons. But many administration officials dismissed his report, including George Tenet, who insisted that despite the report, "I know they had WMD." After David Kay told a reporter,

"I don't think they [WMD] existed," Republican leaders demanded that he testify before the Senate Armed Services Committee. "It turns out we were all wrong..." he told the committee. He told the senators that they found no trucks or factories, no nuclear program, no trailers for the production of biological weapons.

Under interrogation, captured officials with the Iraq Chemical Engineering and Design Center, at which Curveball had claimed to work, all denied knowing him or anything about mobile weapons factories.

Curveball lied to German intelligence officials in order to better his circumstances and to make sure he would be able to remain in Germany. And even though the BND repeatedly warned that Curveball's story was unreliable, US intelligence officials passed it on to the White House, because the Administration was demanding whatever evidence they had on Iraqi WMD, good or bad. The Administrations used the intelligence to further their case for war with Iraq, even though they had been told the information was not reliable and had never been corroborated. No honest and responsible government is going to go to war based on such flimsy and unsubstantiated intelligence.

The Central Intelligence Agency did have another "asset," who was in a much better position to know what was going on in the government of Saddam Hussein than was Curveball. He was no less a personage than Iraq's foreign minister from 2001 to 2003, Naji Sabra. Sabra told the CIA before the invasion that Saddam had stockpiles of chemical weapons (he was mistaken), but that he had no nuclear or biological weapons programs. The CIA was not able to confirm the information from either source. But the Administration preferred to cite the intelligence from Curveball, a total nobody, rather than that from a high government official, because his story fit in better with the Administration's narrative.

NIGERIEN URANIUM ORE

In his now-infamous State of the Union speech of January 2003, George W. Bush not only claimed that Saddam Hussein was producing biological weapons, he also claimed that Saddam was attempting to purchase "significant quantities of uranium from Africa."[59] Bush offered this as evidence that Iraq had an active nuclear weapons program.

As we shall see, there is no doubt that Bush knew the intelligence was based on a forgery.

Bush's claims were based on documents that an Italian intelligence agent had reportedly obtained from someone in the Nigerien embassy in Rome. [60] The documents in question indicated that Iraq had concluded a contract to buy five hundred tons of so-called yellow cake uranium ore from Niger, in West Africa. Yellow cake can be used to make fuel for nuclear power plants, but with different processing, it can also be used in nuclear weapons.

The true origin of the documents has never been established, but some analysts believed that the documents were forged either by British intelligence agents or the CIA. At any rate, the Italian military intelligence agency (SISMI) passed the intelligence along to the CIA. Also, the chief of SISMI took this story directly to then-Deputy National Security Adviser Steven Hadley.

In February 2002, the CIA sent former ambassador Joseph Wilson to Niger to investigate the claims. Wilson had been a diplomat in Niger in the 1970s, and knew many former and current government officials there, and thus had many contacts. These contacts told Wilson that a French-led consortium controlled the two uranium mines in Niger, and it sold its entire output to the French nuclear power industry; it never contracted to sell ore to Iraq. Niger's uranium mines were also tightly controlled by the government; any sale of ore to Iraq would have to have been approved by government officials, which never happened. Wilson met with the US ambassador to Niger, who, to Wilson's surprise, was familiar with the story, and had already reported to Washington that the story was false. Wilson returned to Washington and told the CIA that the intelligence was "unequivocally wrong."[61]

In early 2002 both the CIA and the State Department had also concluded that the documents were falsified. A CIA intelligence brief entitled "Iraq: Nuclear Related Procurement Efforts" reported on the documents. This brief did not make much of the allegations, stating that intelligence was "highly suspect."[62] The deputy commander of US forces in Europe, General Carlton Fulford, Jr., went to Niger and met with its president. Fulford concluded that the report was false, given the tight controls placed on Niger's uranium production and sales. It took the International Atomic Energy Agency only a few hours to conclude that the documents were forged, citing, among other things, the use of incorrect names of Nigerien officials. The Nigerien minister of Foreign Affairs whose name appears on the letterhead of one of the documents had been out of office for more than ten years. Also, the signature on a letter supposedly written by the President of Niger was an obvious forgery.[63]

A CIA official told the BBC that Wilson's report had been passed on to the White House as early as March 2002.[64] In October 2002 CIA Director Tenet called National Security advisor Steve Hadley and asked him to delete the reference to Nigerien yellow cake from a speech Bush was to give in Cincinnati. The CIA sent a follow-up memo to both Hadley and Condoleezza Rice that expressed the CIA's view that the documents were forgeries.

Bush made no reference to Nigerien yellow cake in that speech in Cincinnati in October 2002, but as noted above, he did in his State of the Union speech in January 2003. The Administration later admitted that the story should not have been included in the speech, blaming the "error" on the CIA. But Bush already knew it was a forgery.

This is not the end of the story.

At first Ambassador Wilson was not named in reporting on the yellow cake story. However, Wilson himself wrote an Op-Ed piece in the *New York Times* in July of 2003.[65] After identifying himself as the agent the Administration had sent to Niger, Wilson described his findings and concluded that "intelligence related to Iraq's nuclear weapons program was twisted to exaggerate the Iraqi threat." He also stated that if the Administration deliberately ignored his report, "then a legitimate argument can be made that we went to war under false pretenses."

The Administration was incensed by Wilson's article, and deliberately tried to destroy Joseph Wilson for his temerity in suggesting that the government had misled the public. A week after Wilson's article appeared in the *Times*, *Washington Post* columnist Robert Novak disclosed that Wilson's wife, Valerie Plame, was a CIA operative. This was a devastating revelation, because Plame was an active agent at the time, and her exposure could have endangered not only Plame's life, but also the lives of her associates, contacts, sources, and her operations. Joseph Wilson alleged that this information was leaked to Novak in retaliation for his criticism of the government.

This allegation led to a series of investigations that resulted in the indictment of Vice President Cheney's chief of staff, I. Lewis "Scooter" Libby, for leaking Plame's name to the press. A prominent neo-conservative colleague of Wolfowitz, Rumsfeld, and others, Libby was convicted of perjury and obstruction of justice. He was sentenced to thirty months in jail and a fine of $250,000; George Bush commuted his prison sentence after an appeals court upheld Libby's conviction. Others, including presidential advisor Karl Rove and Undersecretary of State Richard Armitage were linked to the leak of Plame's name. The indictment of Libby asserted that it was Cheney who told his Chief of Staff that Wilson's wife worked for the CIA's Clandestine Service.[66] Whoever it was, George Bush declared that he would fire whoever leaked Plame's identity,[67] but no one ever was fired. Valerie Plame Wilson resigned from the CIA in 2006.

Libby was convicted of perjury and obstruction of justice because he impeded the investigations of the leak. No one has been identified as the leaker, but all the evidence indicates that the White House was indeed involved.

ALUMINUM TUBES

Bush also claimed in his 2003 State of the Union speech that "Our intelligence sources tell us that he has attempted to purchase high-strength aluminum tubes suitable for nuclear weapons production."[68] Once again, Bush was using intelligence that was not solid, and that was contradicted by some analysts.

Iraq did indeed order 60,000 high-strength aluminum tubes, of certain specifications, from a company in Jordan in 2000. These tubes were classified by the United Nations as items forbidden to Iraq under the terms of agreement ending the 1991 Gulf War. The first shipment of these tubes was seized in Jordan by the CIA and the Jordanian secret police. There is no doubt that Saddam Hussein's regime was attempting to purchase proscribed materials. However, there was significant debate among analysts as to Iraq's intended use of these tubes.

CIA agents said that the tubes could be used as rotors in centrifuges that enrich uranium for nuclear weapons. However, the same agents admitted that the tubes could be also be used as casings for artillery rockets.[69] In October 2002, Bush was given a National Intelligence Estimate that stated that the Department of Energy and the State Department Bureau of Intelligence and Research believed "the tubes were intended for use in conventional weapons."[70] According to former Deputy National Security Advisor Stephen Hadley, Bush had been directly and repeatedly warned that there was a big dispute among intelligence analysts as to the purpose of the tubes.

But the Bush Administration, not surprisingly, opted to go with their preferred interpretation, that the tubes were intended for use in producing nuclear weapons, despite the lack of any clear evidence that that was in fact their intended use. In addition to Bush's assertions in his state of the Union speech,

Condoleezza Rice claimed that the tubes "are only suited for nuclear weapons,"[71] even though Rice was surely aware of the debate in the intelligence community regarding the purpose Iraq intended for the aluminum tubes. Cheney and Rumsfeld also trumpeted this "evidence" on *Meet the Press* and *Face the Nation.*

Once again, the Administration "cherry-picked" this intelligence to trot out to the American public as evidence that Saddam Hussein had an active nuclear weapons program, even though they did not know for certain that the aluminum tubes were intended for any such program. They knew there was another interpretation for the evidence, but they chose to ignore that interpretation, and failed to mention it because it would weaken the Administration's claims.

A report by the Select Committee on Intelligence released after the invasion of Iraq concluded that the specifications of the aluminum tubes were unsuitable for use in gas centrifuges, and that they were more likely intended for conventional uses, such as tubes for rockets or mortars. But the damaged had already been done; the Administration had sold its case to the American public, and Bush had his war.

In each of the above cases, the Bush Administration misused the intelligence agencies, politicizing their missions by demanding that the agencies come up with intelligence to back up their claims. Paul Pillar was the CIA's National Intelligence Officer for the Middle East before, during, and after the invasion. In 2006, Pillar wrote an article for *Foreign Affairs* magazine called Intelligence, Policy, and the War in Iraq. Pillar was in a unique position to know just what the intelligence on Iraq was telling us, and he states that "intelligence on Iraqi weapons programs did not drive its decision to go to war," and that "its decision to topple Saddam was driven by other factors."[72] Pillar goes on to say that it was clear to the agencies that the Bush Administration would "frown on or ignore analysis that called into question a decision to go to war...when policymakers repeatedly urge the intelligence community to turn over certain rocks, the process becomes biased." The whole process, as Pillar points out, and as we keep saying, had been turned on its head by Bush and the neoconservatives. They decided to go to war first, and then went looking for intelligence that would justify an invasion.

Terrorist Connections

Perhaps one of the least credible claims made by the Bush Administration was that Saddam Hussein had connections to the al Qaida terrorist group that perpetrated the 9/11 attacks. The charge is ludicrous even just on the face of it; Saddam and al Qaida leader Osama bin Laden were sworn enemies. When Iraq invaded Kuwait in 1990, bin Laden offered to send his mujahedeen fighters from Afghanistan to protect Saudi Arabia from Saddam. Bin Laden also offered support to Islamist rebels in Iraq's Kurdish north. Saddam ran a secular regime; he abolished Quran-based Sharia courts and cracked down on Islamist movements in Iraq. Saddam Hussein was not interested in radical Islam and he considered Osama bin Laden and his jihadist philosophy to be a threat.

Yet both George Bush and Dick Cheney publically claimed that there was a connection between the two. Bush declared in a White House press release in October 2002 that Saddam and bin Laden might conspire to attack the United States.[73] Yet the President's Daily Briefing that Bush received from the CIA on September 21, 2001, stated, "there was scant credible evidence that Iraq had any significant collaborative ties with Al Qaeda."[74] Bush already had the assessment from the CIA regarding Iraq-al Qaida ties, but he chose to ignore it. In fact, he stated, "We have removed an ally of al-Qaida, and cut off a source of terrorist funding" in his address aboard the aircraft carrier *USS Abraham Lincoln* on May 1, 2003, even though by this time he had been told repeatedly that Saddam Hussein had no ties to al Qaida.

As we have seen, Administration officials such as Rumsfeld and Wolfowitz tried to draw a connection between the 9/11 attacks and Saddam Hussein's regime. These alleged connections were always no more than speculation. After exhaustive investigations, US intelligence agencies all concluded that there was no credible evidence of Iraqi involvement in 9/11.

Yet in December of 2001, on the news program *Meet the Press,* Cheney alleged that there had been a meeting between Iraqi officials and Mohammed Atta, the leader of the 9/11 attacks, in Prague, capital of the Czech Republic, five months before the invasion of Iraq. In fact, the FBI actually had evidence that Mohammed Atta was in Florida taking flying lessons at the time of the alleged meetings, and the Iraqi intelligence officer whom Atta supposedly met denied the meeting ever took place.

The story originated with a contact the Czech intelligence agency had in the Iraqi embassy in Prague. This contact claimed, after seeing Atta's picture in the newspaper after 9/11, to have seen the terrorist meeting with the Iraqi official, one Ahmad Samir al-Ani. [75] But in October 2001, the *New York Times* reported that Czech officials were denying that the meeting ever occurred.[76]

Shortly after 9/11, Cheney asked CIA Director Tenet to look into the claims; Tenet reported back in September 2001, "Our Prague office is skeptical about the report." Tenet reported that the evidence suggested that this meeting was highly unlikely.[77] This was three months before Cheney's appearance on *Meet the Press.* Once again, the Administration, knowing that the intelligence was not confirmed, decided to cite the story anyway, because it helped sell their rational for war in Iraq.

Practically every intelligence agency in the United States has since investigated and concluded that the story of an Iraqi-al Qaida meeting in Prague was not true. The 9/11 Commission reported that they had found no evidence of contacts between Saddam and al Qaida or Iraqi involvement in 9/11. An investigation by the US Senate Select Committee on Intelligence found no evidence for a connection between Iraq and al Qaida. But once again, the damage had already been done. The Administration had its war, having done a good job of convincing Americans of their claims. To this day, despite all the evidence to the contrary, many Americans still believe that Saddam Hussein was involved in the 9/11 attacks.

Regime Change

When it became obvious, after the invasion, that Saddam Hussein had no biological weapons, no nuclear weapons program, and no real, active connections to terrorists, the rational for invading Iraq became regime change. The Bush Administration had been calling for the overthrow of Saddam Hussein from the start, but the stated reasons that made his removal necessary had been that he presented an imminent threat to the United States. In the lead-up to the war, the Administration said repeatedly that Saddam was developing biological and/or nuclear weapons, that he had terrorist ties, and that he or his terrorist surrogates might attack us at any time. Remember, both Bush and Condoleezza Rice warned us that we could not wait until the smoking gun came in the form of a mushroom cloud.

But after the regime in Iraq was toppled, weapons inspectors found no weapons of mass destruction and absolutely no evidence of any active WMD development programs. Report after report came out of the intelligence agencies stating declaratively that Saddam had no real, operational relationships with terrorist organizations. The Administration actually began to admit the "intelligence had been wrong."

So then why did we invade Iraq? The message from Bush and company became Iraqi freedom. The Iraqi people needed to be freed from their brutal dictator. And indeed, the list of atrocities committed by Saddam and his regime is very long and sordid; he was a brutally repressive despot who enriched himself and dealt harshly with opponents. As we have seen, he held down the Shiite majority while staffing his government and military with his Sunni allies. His spies were everywhere. There is no question; Saddam Hussein was a murderous tyrant.

But the world is full of murderous tyrants. Just a few examples include North Korea, Sudan, Zimbabwe, Myanmar, Syria, Saudi Arabia, Egypt, and Libya, not to mention Russia. So why Iraq? Why was the freedom of the Iraqi people so important to the United States, and not the freedom of any other people? What was so important about Iraq?

Despite all the claims regarding the imminent danger that Iraq posed to the United States, or the need to free the Iraqi people, the Bush Administration actually had other motives for the invasion, motives that the American people were not likely to support. In any criminal prosecution, the court must consider motivation. It is time to turn our attention to the real motives for these alleged war crimes.

Motivation

A number of alternative motives for the invasion have been proposed. These include a desire for revenge on Saddam Hussein by George W. Bush, seizing Iraqi oil wells, and establishing a long-term US military presence in the Middle East. We will examine each of these possible motives in turn, and assess their likelihood as the real reasons for the US invasion of Iraq.

REVENGE

In 1993, Saddam Hussein allegedly plotted to assassinate George H. W. Bush, the 41st president and father of George W. Bush, during a visit to Kuwait two years after Bush Sr. drove Saddam's forces out of the small Gulf country. A trial ensued in Kuwait, resulting in the conviction of eleven Iraqis and three Kuwaitis. Two of the defendants retracted their confessions; at the time, Human Rights Watch noted that Kuwait habitually coerced confessions from accused criminals. Many observers met the charges with skepticism, including former ambassador Joseph Wilson of Nigerien yellow cake fame.

But the CIA and FBI convinced President Bill Clinton that there was credence to the story, and he ordered a missile strike against Iraqi intelligence headquarters in retaliation, resulting in the deaths of six civilians.[78]

The story led some commentators to speculate that Bush's efforts to topple Saddam Hussein were rooted in a desire for revenge. Bush, speaking at a fundraiser in Houston in September 2002, actually said, "After all, this is the guy who tried to kill my dad."[79] But it is unlikely that revenge was a major motive, although both Bushes possibly got some personal satisfaction from Saddam's overthrow. Even if revenge was one motive for George Bush, it almost certainly was not for all the neo-conservatives in Bush's White House who were active advocates for the invasion. And in all the research done by this investigator, there was no evidence of personal revenge, on the part of George Bush, as a motive for the war with Iraq. We can safely dispense with this subject and move on.

OIL

Following the development of hydraulic fracturing, the United States experienced a boom in oil production, restoring America's position as a major oil producing country. But in the first years of the 21st Century, this was not the case; the United States was heavily dependent on foreign oil, including oil from the Middle East, where the world's largest oil reserves are located; Iraq's proven reserves are the fifth largest in the world.

The Baathist government of Iraq nationalized the oil industry in 1972; oil production was from that point on controlled by the Iraq National Oil Company. "Arab oil for Arabs" was their slogan.[80] "Prior to the 2003 invasion and occupation of Iraq, US and other western oil companies were all but completely shut out of Iraq's oil market," according to oil industry analyst Antonia Juhasz.[81]

Yet the US had a vital, strategic interest in keeping Mideast oil flowing to America. The US military is the single largest consumer of oil products in the world, consuming 100 million barrels per year[82] and access to a steady flow of oil is vitally important to the Pentagon.

President Jimmy Carter avowed in his 1980 State of the Union Address, "An attempt by any outside force to gain control of the Persian Gulf region will be regarded as an assault on the vital interests of the United States of America, and such an assault will be repelled by any means necessary, including military force."[83] Carter made this statement as a warning to the Soviet Union, but government officials have since broadened the meaning of the so-called Carter Doctrine to assert that the US will oppose any attempts to restrict American access to Middle East oil.

Was the invasion of Iraq driven by the Carter Doctrine? It sure sounds like it when you look at remarks made by some Administration officials. The head of US Central Command, General John Abizaid said, "Of course the war is about oil, we can't deny that." Former Senator and Obama Secretary of Defense Chuck Hagel made similar comments. A think tank report from early 2001 recommended that US policy should strive to "ease Iraqi oil field investment restrictions."[84]

The press fulminated almost endlessly about the possibility that the war was all about oil. Articles speculating oil as the real motive were published by CNN, *Newsweek, The Guardian* (UK), and *The Spectator* (UK), just to name a few.

It is also worth noting the connection between the Bush Administration and the oil industry. Both George W. Bush and his father have deep ties to the oil industry. George Bush the elder, the scion of a prominent Connecticut family, moved to Texas in the 1950s and made a lot of money in the oil industry, eventually starting his own company. His son tried his hand in the family business, starting a company called Arbusto (shrub or bush in Spanish), but the company foundered and was eventually acquired by Harken Energy. Both Bushes had oil-industry contracts in the Persian Gulf and ties to the Saudi royal family.

Just prior to becoming vice president, Dick Cheney had been the chief executive of Halliburton, a worldwide oil field services corporation with hundreds of subsidiaries, affiliates and branches. In fact, some critics charge that profits for Halliburton were a prime motivator for Cheney. Indeed, Halliburton subsidiary Kellogg, Brown and Root (KBR) was awarded a $7 billion, no bid contract by the Bush Administration for oil infrastructure work in Iraq just as the war got started. KBR already had a 10-year, open-ended, "cost plus" contract with the Defense Department for logistics work, even though KBR had previously lost the contract for overcharging the Pentagon.[85] In 2001, Halliburton had $427 million in Defense Department contracts; by 2003, they had $4.3 billion.[86]

After Saddam's ouster, the Iraqi oil industry was, indeed, opened to Western oil companies. "Thanks to the invasion and occupation, the companies are now back inside Iraq and producing oil there for the first time since being forced out of the country in 1973," again, according to analyst Antonia Juhasz.[87] Since the invasion, the Iraqi government has signed major oil and gas contracts with several international oil companies, including ExxonMobil, BP, and Royal Dutch Shell.

So it would seem very natural to assume that the invasion was all about maintaining access to that vital resource. But if the real motive was access to Iraqi oil, it would have been cheaper to make a deal with Saddam Hussein rather than invade the country, as many commentators have pointed out. Oil industry experts pointed out that "the expense of the war and occupation would far outweigh any benefit from Iraq's 2.5 million barrels of oil a day."[88]

Oil may not have been the main reason for the invasion, but it was germane to what the prosecution believes was the real motive for the unprovoked war with Iraq.

A LONG-TERM MILITARY PRESENCE

After the invasion and overthrow of Saddam Hussein, the US military began spending huge sums of money upgrading and expanding the bases in Iraq that it occupied. Let's look, for example, at the Balad Air Base, some 45 miles north of Baghdad. Army engineers laid out a plan for improvements and additions to Balad not long after the fall of Baghdad. Contractors, mostly from Kuwait, constructed big new ramps and runway aprons to accommodate huge C-130 cargo planes. The runways were reinforced to handle the C-130s and F-16s. The Pentagon also built four new mess halls, a new recreation facility that included a cybercafé, coffee shop, a Baskin-Robbins ice cream store, an indoor miniature golf course and a movie theater, basketball courts and an auto "dealership" inside the base PX, from which airmen could order a new car for delivery back home. In 2006, Balad Air Base covered 14 square miles and housed some 25,000 Air Force personnel. World wide, air traffic volume at Balad was second only London's Heathrow at that time.

Between Balad and a few other airbases, the US military spent in the neighborhood of $1 billion on upgrades and amenities between 2005 and 2006.

"It's safe to say Balad will be here for a long time," said base commander Brigadier General Frank Gorenc, in 2006. Gorenc said that he was "normalizing" the huge airbase, meaning he was upgrading it to US military specifications.[89] "We will probably be helping the Iraqis [with airpower] for a very long time," he said.

The Bush Administration also spent $592 million to build a new American Embassy in Baghdad. At 104 acres, it is the largest embassy, of any nation, in the world. It includes six apartment buildings, a gym, a movie theater, tennis courts, swimming pool, and its own power, water, and waste facilities.

Both the air bases and the embassy fit in to Donald Rumsfeld's vision for the future of the US military; Rumsfeld envisioned a series of "lily pad" bases around the world where American troops could deploy at a moment's notice.[90] These lily pads would take the place of aircraft carriers. Such bases would be preferable, according to defense analyst Gordon Adams of George Washington University. "There's a huge advantage to land-based infrastructure. At the level of strategy it makes total sense to have Iraqi bases," he said.[91]

General John Abizaid, military commander in Iraqi, told a House subcommittee in 2006 that he could not rule out a long-term military presence in Iraq. "No doubt there is a need for some presence in the region over time," he said, adding that the US and its allies had a vital interest in the region.[92] Former Coalition Provisional Authority leader Jay Garner compared Iraq to the aftermath of the Spanish-American War: "Look back on the Philippines around the turn of the 20th century: they were a coaling station for the navy, and that allowed us to keep a great presence in the Pacific. That's what Iraq is for the next few decades: our coaling station that gives us great presence in the Middle East." [93] A report from the House Appropriations Committee said, "It has become clear in recent years that these expeditionary operations can result in substantial military construction expenditures of a magnitude normally associated with permanent bases."

The establishment of permanent bases in Iraq would not have been without precedent. The United States has often left behind permanently based troops in the wake of previous wars. We still have large numbers of American servicemen and women in Japan, Germany, and South Korea, living and working on large, more-or-less permanent bases. We had large bases in the Philippines until the Philippine government refused to renew their leases. And we would no doubt still have large bases in Vietnam, such as we had at Da Nang and Cam Ranh Bay, if we hadn't lost that war.

Facing criticism from the press and Congress over all the infrastructure spending in Iraq, Bush and other Administration officials denied that they intended a long-term US military presence in Iraq, despite the fact that Bush had already said that the final number of troops in Iraq "will be decided by future presidents." Donald Rumsfeld ducked the question, saying, when asked about permanent bases, that it would be up to the Iraqi government.

On the other hand, people like ambassador to Iraq Zalmay Khalilzad denied the US was seeking long term bases; General Anthony Zinni said such bases would be a "stupid" idea. Bush advisor Karen Hughes said on the *Charlie Rose Show,* "We want to bring our people home as soon as possible."

Did the Bush Administration plan for a long-term American military presence in Iraq, or not? Despite the assertions and vague denials from the Bush government, there is very strong evidence that the Bush neoconservatives did indeed carry out the invasion of Iraq with the intent of establishing a virtually permanent military presence in Iraq as part of a larger strategy to project American power around the world.

PROJECTING AMERICAN POWER: PNAC

Vice President Dick Cheney and his circle of closest advisors were interested in regime change in Iraq as far back as Cheney's stint as Secretary of Defense under the first President Bush. When Saddam Hussein invaded Kuwait in 1991, Cheney argued that we should take out the Iraq dictator, since our military was already in the region. George H. W. Bush, a more cautious man than his son, vetoed any such notions. But Cheney didn't drop the idea. In 1992, Cheney produced a Defense Planning Guidance document that was drafted largely by his advisors Paul Wolfowitz and "Scooter" Libby.[94] The plan called for an expanded US military presence throughout the world, including in the Middle East. The paper stated, "In the Middle East and Southwest Asia, our overall objective is to remain the predominant power in the region and preserve US and western access to the region's oil."

The plan was widely criticized, and it became moot when Bush lost his bid for reelection in 1992. However, the authors of the Defense Planning Guidance did not give up on the policy proposals contained in the document.

In 1997, William Kristol, publisher of the conservative magazine *The Weekly Standard*, and Robert Kagan, a leading neoconservative, founded a think tank called The Project for a New American Century (PNAC). PNAC's Statement of Principles, a kind of neoconservative manifesto, declared that the United States needed "a military that is strong and ready to meet both present and future challenges; a foreign policy that boldly and purposefully promotes American principles abroad; and national leadership that accepts the United States' global responsibilities." This statement also said that "it is important to shape circumstances before crises emerge," and that "extending an international order friendly to our security, our prosperity, and our principles" should be the major focus of American foreign policy.[95] The Statement of Principles recommended a significant increase in military spending in order to fulfill America's "responsibilities of global leadership."

Signatories to PNAC's Statement of Principles include, among others, several people we have become familiar with in this narrative: Dick Cheney, Zalmay Khalilzad, Lewis Libby, Donald Rumsfeld, and Paul Wolfowitz. These men formed the core of the neoconservative cadre within the George W. Bush administration, and they were the biggest proponents of deposing Saddam Hussein.

In 2000, PNAC published a position paper entitled "Rebuilding America's Defenses."[96] Its principal author was Thomas Donnelly, a former congressional staffer, working from pieces written by various authors, including Lewis Libby and Paul Wolfowitz. This seventy-five-page document proposes a very aggressive projection of American power around the world. Noting that the United States was the world's only remaining superpower, the paper says, "America's grand strategy should aim to preserve and extend this advantageous position as far into the future as possible." The introduction also states that the paper builds upon the Defense Policy Guidance, the set of proposals drafted by Libby and Wolfowitz in 1992 for then-Defense Secretary Dick Cheney.

The paper called for the US to maintain its nuclear superiority, to expand military strength, and, significantly, to "reposition US forces to respond to 21st Century strategic realities." This document even seriously called for the militarization of outer space and the creation of a new branch of the military called the US Space Forces, devoting several pages to the topic. This is despite the fact that the United States is a signatory to treaties outlawing the militarization of space.[97]

Rebuilding America's Defenses claimed that our military was woefully unprepared for future challenges, saying that there was "no shortage of powers...who have taken the collapse of the Soviet empire as an opportunity to...challenge the American-led security order." A few paragraphs later, the authors claim that "adversaries like Iraq...are rushing to develop ballistic missiles and nuclear weapons as a deterrent to American intervention in regions they seek to dominate." Like the Bush Administration's claims, these assertions were not backed up by any evidence.

Under a section titled "Repositioning Today's Force," the position paper asserts, "The presence of American forces in critical regions around the world is the visible expression of the extent of America's status as a superpower. It will be difficult, if not impossible, to sustain the role of global guarantor without a substantial overseas presence." Referring to the no-fly zones that the US had been enforcing in Iraq since the 1991 Gulf War, the paper goes on to say that the Air Force represents the "long-term commitment of the United States and its major allies to a region of vital importance." Elsewhere, this call to arms says America needs a network of forward operating bases in order to "project force to outlying regions," and that the Army should have a "permanent unit ...based in the Persian Gulf region." Regarding the Air Force, this document recommends that "Independent, expeditionary air wings...should be based in the Persian Gulf [among other places]. The Air Force presence in the Gulf Region is a vital one...and the United States should consider it a *de facto* permanent presence."

The following two sentences are at the heart of the prosecution's case regarding the Bush Administrations real motives for invading Iraq. "Indeed, the United States has sought for decades to play a more permanent role in Gulf regional security. While the unresolved conflict with Iraq provides the immediate justification, the need for a substantial American force presence in the Gulf transcends the issue of the regime of Saddam Hussein."

"A more permanent role;" that quotation speaks for itself. The word "permanent" pops up repeatedly throughout the document. "The unresolved conflict with Iraq" clearly indicates that bad guy Saddam Hussein provides the rationale for invading Iraq, as opposed to some other Middle East country. The second half of the sentence needs translation. The authors are saying that, because of its disruptive and repressive dictator, the logical place to establish that permanent presence is Iraq, but that it would still be the logical choice even if Saddam Hussein were no longer in power. A few pages later, the paper says, "From an American perspective, the value of such bases would endure even should Saddam Hussein pass from the scene."

Finally, this position paper suggested that achieving the goal of establishing a significant global military presence might require a "catastrophic and catalyzing event–like a new Pearl Harbor." An event something like the September 11, 2001, terrorist attacks.

Conclusions

The neoconservative Bush Administration went to war, not over weapons of mass destruction, or to eliminate a threat to the United States, or to liberate the Iraqis, or even to rid the world of Saddam Hussein, as they claimed. They went to war with the intention of establishing a long-term American military presence in the Middle East as part of a larger plan to project American power around the world. The 9/11 terrorist attacks gave them the opportunity they needed to pursue their goals.

INDICTMENT

They did not find evidence indicating Iraq was threatening us, and then act upon it. They wanted to go to war, for their own reasons, and then trumped up charges against the regime of Saddam Hussein. And they relied on unsubstantiated or downright fabricated intelligence to back up their claims. They trumpeted these claims to the public repeatedly in a cynical effort to convince us that we faced a dire and immediate threat, when no threat of any kind actually existed. The Bush Administration lied about the need to invade Iraq, and they lied about their motives for the invasion.

They lied to us, and many, many people have paid the price. But the culprits have not.

May it please the court, the prosecution rests its case.

CLOSING ARGUMENTS

L adies and gentlemen of the jury:
        Richard Cheney said many things during the run-up to the Iraq War. Many of his claims and assertions, as we have seen, were false, but there is one thing he said that he may really have believed; he said we would be welcomed as liberators. Cheney and his colleagues believed it would be a cakewalk, which the invasion and defeat of the Iraqi army actually were. But securing the peace turned out to be a much more difficult problem. Instead of deliriously happy Iraqis waving American flags and throwing flowers to the soldiers as they entered Baghdad, they started shooting at them almost as soon as they arrived. The newly liberated Iraqis were not about to allow us to keep a contingent of soldiers in Iraq indefinitely.

Of course, we know Cheney was wrong about how we would be received.

What Cheney failed to anticipate, along with everyone else in the White House, was the sectarian hostility that our invasion unleashed, along with the deep resentment toward US troops, who were seen, not as liberators, but as the invaders and occupation force that they actually were. This failure to consider the history, culture, and politics of the region led directly to a huge quagmire that took years of blood and treasure to extract ourselves from. Anyone with even a passing knowledge of Iraq would have known that, because of the Sunni/Shiite divide in Iraq, toppling Saddam Hussein would probably lead to sectarian strife, if not outright civil war. There had to have been at least a few voices in the White House calling for the Administration to slow down and think about the possible consequences of such precipitate action. But if there was, those voices went unheeded in the headlong rush to accomplish something the Bush neoconservatives adamantly intended to do.

If things had gone as Cheney and the others had anticipated, that is, if we had been welcomed as liberators by the Sunnis, Shiites, and Kurds, there may not have been the chaos, rioting, and violence that ensued. But, in their ignorance and hubris, their rush to demonstrate American power, the Bush Administration directly and deliberately led us into an unmitigated disaster.

It is difficult to determine exactly what the war in Iraq cost American taxpayers, but one estimate placed the dollar figure north of $1 trillion, and that the war added $1 trillion to the national debt. More importantly, the war cost some 4,490 Americans their lives; another 32,226 were wounded. On the bright side, big advances in battlefield medicine meant that over 90 percent of the wounded survived their injuries. On the down side, that means many veterans will be dealing with severe disabilities for the rest of their lives. Caring for these brave veterans is an expense that must be added to what the Pentagon spent prosecuting the war.

Additionally, we must consider the social cost of the casualties, the shattered and grieving families, the lost potential of the disabled, the post-traumatic stress that so many veterans must cope with.

This war was very costly for America, and the costs are immeasurably compounded by the knowledge that this war, a war that did not have to be fought, was sold to the American public on false pretenses. The war was a tragedy compounded by a travesty.

And we have not even begun to tabulate the costs to Iraq and the Middle East in general. Estimates vary widely, but many sources put the number of Iraqis killed in the invasion and succeeding violence at around 170,000, with other estimates in the neighborhood of half a million. An estimated 250,000 more were wounded. The invasion and ensuing chaos also created thousands of orphaned children and nearly four million refuges.

The invasion, the dismissal of the entire Iraqi government, and the subsequent sectarian violence left Iraq in ruins. Oil production, which was supposed to help pay for the war, did not recover to pre-war levels until 2009. However, the ISIS take-over of parts of northern Iraq meant a loss of control over much of the country's oil fields. The economy is in ruins. Government is weak and ineffective. And terrorists still control large areas of the country.

Is your average Iraqi better off without Saddam Hussein? The most positive answer one can give is "not yet."

What's more, a convincing argument can be made that the current, widespread disorder in the Middle East (Syria, the Islamic State) can be directly attributed to the American invasion and subsequent destabilization of Iraq.

All this death and destruction would never have happened if the George W. Bush Administration had not been so foolish, arrogant, reckless, and dishonest, as to start a pre-emptive war with a country that was, in reality, not threatening the United States, either directly or indirectly.

We have shown that the Bush Administration was filled with people, the so-called neoconservatives, who were gunning for Saddam Hussein before they were even in office. We have shown that they were looking for an excuse to overthrow the Iraqi dictator from the first weeks of the Bush Administration. And we have shown that after 9/11, they felt that they had their excuse, and advocated striking Iraq as well as al-Qaida and the Afghan Taliban.

We have also shown that many of the people accused in this indictment were members of an organization, the Project for a New American Century, that advocated the projection of American military power around the world, and that they singled out Iraq as a logical place for basing American troops, whether or not they had to overthrow Saddam Hussein to do so.

We have shown that the George W. Bush Administration decided to start a war, and then went looking for a rationale that they could sell to the American people, rather than responding to any actual threats to the United States from Iraq. We have shown that they orchestrated a full-court press propaganda campaign in order to convince the American people of an imminent threat that in fact did not exist.

Their claims that Iraq was amassing weapons of mass destruction were based entirely on bad intelligence that they had been warned had not been corroborated and was not reliable. Their claims that Saddam Hussein planned to use these WMD against the United States were entirely fabricated. In fact, many intelligence analysts, in the US and around the world, believed that Saddam had been "put in a box" after the 1991 Gulf War, and that he was really no threat to anyone.

If the Administration had only claimed that Saddam Hussein was a brutal dictator who terrorized his own people while suppressing the Shiite majority, there would have been no dispute. But that was not sufficient to frighten the American people into supporting a war with Iraq. The Bush neocons cynically took advantage of the 9/11 terrorist attacks to link Saddam to the very real threats that Americans were facing. They wanted to scare people into accepting a war with a nation that really was not threatening us, and they succeeded.

As we have shown, the purported threats from Iraq did not actually exist. We have also shown that Bush et al. first made the claims of weapons of mass destruction, and then leaned on the intelligence services, mainly the CIA, to find evidence to back up their claims. Or as former CIA National Intelligence Officer for the Near East Paul Pillar put it, the administration used intelligence not to inform decision-making, but to justify a decision already made. We have also shown that the Administration made their accusations after, not before, the intelligence services warned them not to use the intelligence in their public statements.

Even if no one ever told George Bush or Dick Cheney to their face that the intelligence they cited was false or could not be corroborated, we have shown that the intelligence services made every attempt to warn the Administration that the "intelligence" they had was not reliable. If Bush and company were ignorant of the real status of the intelligence, it was willful ignorance. Again, this was an administration that was intent on invading Iraq, and it went looking for excuses to give the American people, since their real motives would not have been met with approval. Too many people would have objected to Bush's real designs on Iraq, so they had to manufacture stories of a threat that didn't exist.

And in the final analysis, it doesn't really matter whether Bush and company knew the intelligence was bad or not. They said they *knew* Saddam Hussein had WMD, when, in fact, there were no WMD or weapons programs in Iraq. They said we had to attack now, before it was too late, when there was, in fact, no urgency, and the Administration knew it. Even if they had found weapons of mass destruction after the invasion, they would still be guilty of lying to the American public about their real reasons for the invasion.

We have shown that those real–and hidden–reasons for the Iraq War were reasons that Dick Cheney, Donald Rumsfeld, Paul Wolfowitz, and others had been advocating for several years before George Bush became president. Neoconservative philosophy held that the United States, in order to preserve and enhance its standing as the only remaining superpower in the world, should project American military power around the world. The Project for a New American Century, of which the above-mentioned individuals were members, called for America to establish a long-term military presence around the world, including the Middle East, and that they identified Iraq as the logical place, whether Saddam Hussein was still in power or not. PNAC's document Rebuilding America's Defenses also declared that it might take a big event–like Pearl Harbor–to present the United States with the opportunity to carry out this plan; 9/11 provided the Bush Administration with its Pearl Harbor.

So why do we not have those permanent bases in Iraq if that is what the war in Iraq was all about? Two reasons: first, the unanticipated insurgency and attacks on US forces kept the Administration's hands tied; they never did gain control over the country. Secondly, George Bush was succeeded by a Democrat who pledged during his campaign to end the war in Iraq. If a Republican had followed Bush into the White House, we would probably still be in Iraq today.

What kind of government would deliberately mislead the nation into supporting a war of choice–not a war of necessity–by falsely claiming that we faced imminent danger from a nation that was not presenting any threat of any kind? What kind of government decides to invade another country and then uses suspect intelligence to justify the invasion? What kind of government repeatedly lies to its citizens in order to achieve their foreign policy goals? What kind of government is willing to risk the lives of a great many people, both American and Iraqi, just so that the United States could demonstrate its superiority by flexing its military muscles?

The answer is a deeply dishonest government; a criminal government that believed the ends justified the means. A government so filled with hubris and belief in the supremacy of American power that they were willing to lie to the public in order to demonstrate that power to the world. A government so dogmatic about its ideology that it ignored the very real potential for the violence, chaos, and sectarian warfare that Saddam's overthrow unleashed.

To top it off, they launched this ill-advised adventure when we were already involved in another war, a war to defeat the real perpetrators of 9/11 and the criminal regime that sheltered them. Thus the Bush Administration shifted its attention away from Afghanistan and the truly vital mission of eliminating Osama bin Laden and al Qaida. This, also, was such a bad strategic decision that it, too, rises to the level of a criminal act. The conflict in Afghanistan drags on to this day, with no resolution in sight.

Given the evidence that the war in Iraq was a war of choice based on trumped up charges, to achieve dubious policy goals that were not shared with the public, while dropping the ball on the arguably more necessary war in Afghanistan, the verdict the jury must return is obvious. Given that a great many people died, billions of dollars were wasted, and an entire region was devastated, all because George Bush, Dick Cheney, et al. misled the nation, there is only one verdict that can be reached.

Guilty as charged. Your verdict is the judgment of history.

INDICTMENT

employ any critical thinking or ask to see the evidence that the Administration claimed to have. We acted out of fear, and therefore acted irrationally. We must resolve to better hold our government leaders accountable in the future. We cannot allow ourselves to be stampeded into this kind of debacle ever again.

Never, ever, again.

INDICTMENT

APPENDIX: THE DEFENDANTS

George W. Bush, President of the United States

George Walker Bush is the oldest son of former President George Herbert Walker Bush. The younger Bush earned a bachelor's degree in history from Yale University in 1968. After an undistinguished stint in the Texas Air National Guard, he earned an MBA from Harvard. Bush dabbled rather unsuccessfully in the oil business, then became a co-owner of the Texas Rangers baseball team. He was elected governor of Texas in 1994 and won reelection in 1998. He became president after winning one of the most contested elections in US history.

It is the considered opinion of this writer that George W. Bush is a fairly shallow person, and as such had no native, deeply held political philosophy of his own. Therefore, he was malleable and thus willing to adopt the neo-conservative policy positions, and consequently lead the nation into an unprovoked war. According to the Iraq on the Record report of the US House Committee on Government Reform, Bush made a total of fifty-five misleading statements regarding the threat posed by Iraq, between September 2002 and July 2003.

Richard B. Cheney, Vice President of the United States

Richard Bruce Cheney has been a conservative actor in American politics since the administration of Richard Nixon, where he was an aide to Economic Opportunity Office Director Donald Rumsfeld. Under Nixon's successor, Gerald Ford, Cheney became Deputy Chief of Staff, then Chief of Staff. He chaired Ford's unsuccessful election campaign of 1976. Cheney then spent ten years in the House of Representatives, where he compiled one of the most conservative records of any congressman. He became Secretary of Defense under George H.W. Bush; when Bush lost his reelection bid, Cheney moved to the private sector. He was the head of the Halliburton Corporation from 1995 to 2000. In 2000, he was named to head

George W. Bush's vice presidential candidate search; Cheney wound up nominating himself.

As we have seen, Dick Cheney was interested in toppling Saddam Hussein since the 1991 Gulf War. Cheney was essentially the ringleader of the neoconservative clique in the White House. According to the Iraq on the Record report, Cheney made fifty-one misleading statements about Iraq between March 2002 and January 2004.

Donald Rumsfeld, Secretary of Defense

Donald Henry Rumsfeld began his political career in the House of Representatives, where he served three terms. He was appointed director of the Office of Economic Opportunity by Richard Nixon; under Gerald Ford he was first Chief of Staff and then was appointed the country's youngest ever Secretary of Defense. After the Ford Administration, Rumsfeld worked in the private sector; he returned to the office of Defense Secretary under George W. Bush in 2001.

As a signatory to the Project for a New American Century's Statement of Principles, Rumsfeld was among the leading advocates of a long-term American military presence in the Middle East. Iraq on the Record states that Rumsfeld made fifty-two misleading statements between May 2002 and November 2003.

Condoleezza Rice, National Security Advisor

Condoleezza Rice earned a PhD from the University of Denver in 1981; from there she went on to teach at Stanford University. After a brief stint with the National Security Council, Rice was named as Provost at Stanford in 1993. Rice served as a foreign policy advisor to the George W. Bush campaign; after he won, she was named to the office of National Security Advisor.

Although Rice is not the worst offender in the Bush Administration, she also made a number of misleading statements–twenty-nine, according to the Iraq on the Record report, including the infamous mushroom cloud statement. Rice, as much as anybody in the White House, should have known exactly how reliable the intelligence on Iraqi WMD was; interpreting intelligence was her job. But that didn't keep her from making demonstrably false statements.

Colin Powell, Secretary of State

Colin Luther Powell was a career military man; his thirty-five years of service included tours in Vietnam and South Korea. He became Ronald Reagan's National Security Advisor in 1987. In 1989 Powell was appointed Chairman of the Joint Chiefs of Staff, the highest position in the military; he was Chairman during the 1991 Gulf War. In 2001 Powell became George W. Bush's Secretary of State.

Colin Powell was a much more moderate Republican than most of the rest of the Bush White House, and his colleagues often accused him of "not being on board." He was not a member of the neoconservative clique, and if there was any voice of moderation in the Administration, it was Powell. However, he still helped sell the war to the public, making some fifty misleading statements regarding the threat posed by Saddam Hussein, according to the Iraq on the Record report.

Paul Wolfowitz, Assistant Secretary of Defense

Paul Dundes Wolfowitz earned a PhD in Political Science from the University of Chicago in 1972 and subsequently taught at Yale University. He joined the State Department under Ronald Reagan, who appointed him ambassador to Indonesia in 1986. At the time, Wolfowitz already was developing his philosophy that the United States should actively promote western-style democracy around the world. Wolfowitz moved to the Defense Department under George H.W. Bush, as Undersecretary for Policy. After a stint at Johns Hopkins University, Wolfowitz rejoined the Defense Department as an Assistant Secretary in 2001.

Paul Wolfowitz was not one of the primary shills selling the war in Iraq to the American public. He was, however, the coauthor of the 1991 Defense Planning Guidance document, a signatory to the Project for a New American Century, and a contributor to that organization's paper Rebuilding America's Defenses. As such, Wolfowitz was one of the prime neoconservative advocates for deposing Saddam Hussein and occupying Iraq. As Assistant Secretary of Defense, he was one of the prime architects of the war.

The following individuals were more or less minor players in the Bush Administration's plan to sell and then prosecute a preemptive, unprovoked war with Iraq. They are, nonetheless, also culpable.

Douglas Feith, Undersecretary of Defense for Policy

As an assistant to Wolfowitz, Feith helped set up the Office of Special Plans to dig up any actionable intelligence on Iraq and helped to plan the war.

I. Lewis Libby, Chief of Staff to Vice President Cheney

Libby was a former student of Wolfowitz; he thus became a leading neoconservative who, as coauthor of the 1991 Defense Planning Guidance, helped develop the Bush Administration policy regarding Iraq.

Richard Armitage, Deputy Secretary of State

Armitage was one of the neoconservative activists who wrote to President Bill Clinton in 1998 urging him to overthrow Saddam Hussein. He also was implicated as the leaker in the Valery Plame affair.

Karl Rove, Senior Advisor to the President

Rove had been an advisor to George W. Bush since Bush's unsuccessful congressional campaign in 1978. Rove also was not a primary mouthpiece for the Administration's campaign to sell the war. He was, however, a very willing participant in the deception.

SOURCES

1 Holguin, Jaime, CBS News, 3/22/03

2 President's Remarks at the United Nations General Assembly, http://georgewbush-whitehouse.archives.gov/news/releases/2002/09/20020912-1.html, accessed 3/20/16.

3 Blitzer, Wolf, *Search for the Smoking Gun,* CNN.com, 1/10/2003. Accessed 3/29/16.

4 Authorization for Use of Military Force Against Iraq Resolution of 2002; Public Law 107-243–Oct 16, 2002. US Government Publishing Office.

5 Blix, Hans, *Thirteenth quarterly report of the Executive Chairman of the United Nations Monitoring, Verification and Inspection Commission in accordance with paragraph 12 of Security council resolution 1284 (1999)*, UNMOVIC, 5/13/2003.

6 *The Battle of Nasiriyah,* Wikipedia.org, accessed 3/29/16.

7 House, Billy, and Shaffer, Mark, "Mom, Hopi, hero: Piestewa an icon," *Arizona Republic*, 4/10/2003.

8 Zucchino ,David, Thunder Run: The Armored Strike to Capture Baghdad, 3/22/2004.

9 Text of Bush Speech, CBS News, May 1, 2003, cbsnews.com, accessed 4/7/2016.

10 *Meet the Press,* NBC, 3/16/2003.

11 Zakaria, Fareed, Prizes for Bad Diplomacy, *Newsweek*, 3/31/2003.

12 Barry, John, and Thomas, Evan, The Unbuilding of Iraq, Newsweek, 10/6/2003.

13 Hirsh, Michael, Nordland, Rod, and Hoseball, Mark, About Face in Iraq, *Newsweek*, 11/24/2003.

14 ibid.

15 Iraqi Insurgency Groups: globalsecurity.org, accessed 9/13/2016.

16 iCasualties: OIF - Deaths by IED. Archived 1/13/2009 at the Wayback Machine.

17 Ricks, Thomas E. *Fiasco: The American Military Adventure in Iraq*, Penguin Books. 2007.

18 Woodward, Bob. *State of Denial*, Simon & Shuster, New York. 2006

[19] President George W. Bush (January 10, 2007). "President's Address to the Nation"

[20] Biddle, Stephen, Friedman, Jeffrey A., and Shapiro, Jacob N, Testing the Surge: Why Did Violence Decline in Iraq in 2007?, *International Security*. **37** (1): 7–40, 07/1/2012.

[21] Paley, Amit R., Shift in Tactics Aims to revive Struggling Insurgency, *Washington Post*, 2/8/2008.

[22] Flaherty, Anne and Loven, Jennifer, Exit Date Vetoed, so Dems Mull Benchmarks, Associated Press, quoted in the Arizona Daily Sun 5/2/2007.

[23] Documented civilian deaths from violence, Iraqbodycount.org. Accessed 09/28/2016.

[24] Woodward, Bob, *State of Denial; Bush at War, Part III*, Simon & Schuster, New York, 2006.

[25] ibid.

[26] Nichols, John, *Dick; the Man Who Is President*, The New Press, New York, 2004.

[27] Drogin, Bob, *Curveball: Spies, Lies and the Con Man Who Caused a War*, Random House, New York, 2007.

[28] President Bush in a speech in Cincinnati, Ohio, 10/7/2002; quoted at cfr.org, "Iraq: Justifying the War." Accessed 10/4/2016.

[29] Speech to the United Nations, 2/5/2003; full text on the Guardian.com. Accessed 10/4/2016.

[30] State of the Union Speech, 1/28/2003. Full text on Washingtonpost.com. Accessed 10/4/2016.

[31] Presidential speech; whitehouse.gov/news/releases/2002/10/print/20021007-8.html. Accessed 10/25/2005.

[32] Ibid.

[33] Rumsfeld Briefing on military activity, 3/25/2003. Archived by AP 7/21/2015. https://www.youtube.com/watch?v=ZgS6JggWtgE. Accessed 2/23/2017.

[34] *The Vice President Appears on NBC's Meet the Press*, White House press release, The White House, 12/9/2001.

[35] President Bush in a speech in Cincinnati, Ohio, 10/7/2002; quoted at cfr.org, "Iraq: Justifying the War." Accessed 10/4/2016.

[36] Open Letter to the President, 2/19/98. Quoted on Iraqwatch.org, accessed 10/14/2016.

[37] Suskind, Ron. *The Price of Loyalty.* Simon & Shuster, New York, 2004.

[38] Ibid.

[39] Ibid.

[40] "Building Momentum for Regime Change: Rumsfeld's Secret Memos, msnbc.com. Accessed 11/18/2016.

[41] Clarke, Richard A. *Against All Enemies.* Free Press, New York, 2004.

[42] Hersh, Seymour M., Selective Intelligence, *The New Yorker*, 5/5/2003.

[43] "Operation Southern Focus" Wikipedia.org. Accessed 11/18/2016.

[44] van Natta Jr., Don, Bush Was Set on Path to War, Memo by British Adviser Says, *New York Times*, 3/27/2006.

[45] Presidential speech; whitehouse.gov/news/releases/2002/10/print/20021007-8.html. Accessed 10/25/2005.

[46] Special Investigations Division, US House Committee on Government Reform, *Iraq on the Record*, 3/16/2004.

[47] McClellan, Scott, *What Happened: Inside the Bush White House*, Public Affairs, New York, 2008.

[48] Rampton, Sheldon and Stauber, John, *Weapons of Mass Deception: The Uses of Propaganda in Bush's War on Iraq*, Penguin Group, New York, 2003.

[49] Woodward, Bob, *Plan of Attack*, Simon and Schuster, New York, 2004.

[50] Thirteenth quarterly report of the Executive Chairman of the United Nations Monitoring, Verification and Inspection Commission, United Nations Security Council, 5/30/2003. Accessed at un.org, 3/8/2017.

[51] Associated Press, *Wolfowitz Comments Revive Doubts Over Iraq's WMD*, 5/30/2003. Accessed on usatoday.com 3/8/2017.

[52] Pillar, Paul R., *Intelligence, Policy and the Iraq War*, Foreign Affairs, March/April 2006.

[53] Nichols, John, *Dick; the Man Who Is President*, The New Press, New York, 2004.

[54] Gompert, David C., Binnendijk, Hans, and Lin, Bonny, The Iraq War: Bush's Biggest Blunder, *Newsweek*, 12/25/2014.

[55] Drogin, Bob, *Curveball: Spies, Lies and the Con Man Who Caused a War*, Random House, New York, 2007.

[56] State of the Union Speech, 1/28/2003. Full text on Washingtonpost.com. Accessed 10/4/2016.

[57] Warrick, Joby, Lacking Biolabs, Trailers Carried Case for War, *Washington Post*, 4/12/2006.

58 Interview with Charles Duelfer, "Iraq WMD Find Did Not Point to Ongoing Program", NPR Talk of the Nation, June 22, 2006.

59 State of the Union Speech, 1/28/2003. Full text on Washingtonpost.com. Accessed 10/4/2016.

60 Rufford, Nicholas, Italian spies 'faked documents' on Saddam nuclear purchase, *The Sunday Times of London*, 8/1/2004.

61 Kristof, Nicholas D., Missing in Action: Truth, *The New York Times*, 5/6/2003

62 Report on the U.S. Intelligence Community's Prewar Intelligence Assessments on Iraq, Senate Select Committee on Intelligence, 2004.

63 Hersh, Seymour M., Who Lied to Whom?, *The New Yorker*, 3/31/2003.

64 News.bbc.co.uk, *White House "warned over Iraq claim*, 7/9/2003, accessed 2/2/2017.

65 Wilson, Joseph C., What I Didn't Find in Africa, *The New York Times*, 7/6/2003.

66 Thomas, Evan, Cheney's Cheney, *Newsweek*, 11/7/2005.

67 Isikoff, Michael, The Leaker in Chief?, *Newsweek*, 4/4/ 2006.

68State of the Union Speech, 1/28/2003. Full text on Washingtonpost.com. Accessed 10/4/2016.

69 *Spinning the Tubes*, Australian Broadcasting Corporation, 2003.

70 Waas, Murray, What Bush Was Told About Iraq, *National Journal*, 3/2/2006.

71 *Top Bush officials push case against Saddam*, CNN.com, 9/8/2002

72 Pillar, Paul R., Intelligence, Policy and the Iraq War, *Foreign Affairs*, March/April 2006.

73 *President Bush Outlines Iraqi Threat*, White House news release, The White House, 10/7/2002.

74 Key Bush Intelligence Briefing Kept From Hill Panel, *National Journal*, 11/22/2005.

75 Atta in Prague? An Iraqi prisoner holds the answer to this 9/11 mystery, *The Wall Street Journal*, 11/22/2005

76 http://www.nytimes.com/2001/10/20/world/a-nation-challenged-terrorism-trail-no-evidence-suspect-met-iraqi-in-prague.html. Accessed 2/7/2017.

77 Suskind, Ron, *The One Percent Doctrine*, Simon and Schuster, New York, 2006, pg. 23.

[78] Lobe, Jim, *So, Did Saddam Hussein Try to Kill Bush's Dad?* IPSnews.net, 10/18/2004. Accessed 2/10/2017.

[79] King, John, *Bush Calls Saddam "the Guy Who Tried to Kill My Dad,"* CNN.com/inside Politics, Posted 9/7/2002. Accessed 2/10/2017.

[80] *Why you can't explain the Iraq war without mentioning oil,* TheConversation.com 6/8/16. Accessed 2/11/2017.

[81] Jamail, Dahr, *Western Oil Firms Remain as US Exits Iraq,* Aljazeera.com, 1/7/2012. Accessed 2/11/2017.

[82] *The U.S. Military and Oil,* Union of Concerned Scientists, ucsusa.org. Accessed 2/12/2017.

[83] Bacevich, Andrew J., *The Carter Doctrine at 30,* Worldaffairsjournal.org, 4/1/2010. Accessed 2/11/2017.

[84] Jaffe, Amy Myers, Project Director, *Strategic Energy Policy Challenges for the 21st Century,* James A. Baker III Institute for Public Policy and the Council on Foreign Relations.

[85] Hess, Pamela, *Halliburton: $9.6 Billion in Iraq So Far,* United Press International, 2/25/2005.

[86] Phillips, Peter, *Is US Military Dominance of the World a Good Idea?* Commondreams.org, 2/9/2006. Accessed 2/9/2006.

[87] Jamail, Dahr, *Western Oil Firms Remain as US Exits Iraq,* Aljazeera.com, 1/7/2012. Accessed 2/11/2017.

[88] Hirsh, Michael, Blood, Oil & Iraq, *Newsweek,* 3/10/2003.

[89] Hirsh, Michael, Stuck in the Hot Zone, *Newsweek,* 5/1/2006.

[90] Ibid.

[91] *Extended Presence of US in Iraq Looms Large,* Associate Press, 3/21/2006.

[92] Allen, Vicki, *Abizaid Says US May Want to Keep Bases in Iraq,* Reuters, 3/15/2006.

[93] National Journal; quoted in *Bush Lies Uncovered,* alternet.org, 2/22/2004. Accessed 2/18/2017.

[94] Nichols, John, *Dick: The Man Who Is President,* The New Press, New York, 2004.

[95] Project for a New American Century, *Statement of Principles,* 6/3/1997. Archived on rrojasddatabank.info, accessed 2/18/2017.

[96] Donnelly, Thomas, principal author, *Rebuilding America's Defenses,* Project for a New American Century, 9/2000.

[97] Treaty on Principles Governing the Activities of States in the Exploration and Use of Outer Space, including the Moon and Other Celestial Bodies, United Nations Office for Outer Space Affairs.